Getting Old

Getting Old offers concise advice and practical suggestions for all readers interested in or worried about ageing, either in themselves or in someone they care about. With a focus on a positive view of ageing, it discusses central physical and mental aspects of getting old, as well as the social and psychological aspects such as choosing where to live and becoming more oneself.

Rowan Bayne and Carol Parkes take a pragmatic approach to reviewing what is happening in many aspects of your life as you age. Essential topics covered include mobility; diet and digestion; understanding and improving sleep; memory problems and dementia; being an active participant in consultations about your own healthcare; attitudes to getting old; romantic relationships and loneliness; deciding where to live, moving house and choosing other types of living arrangements; and death and grief. They invite readers to focus on their own life and experience, to understand who they are and what they really want now. An important part of self-understanding is the application of personality theory to changes associated with getting old, and readers are encouraged to reflect on what might work for people with their personality characteristics, and how to improve their stress management, communication and decision making.

With suggestions for further reading and useful organisations that offer support, *Getting Old* offers valuable, affirming guidance for all those and their relatives going through this life stage, as well as health, social care and counselling students and professionals.

Rowan Bayne is Emeritus Professor of Psychology and Counselling at the University of East London. His main expertise is in applied personality theory, counselling and counsellor training. He has published 18 books and has run courses on selection interviewing, personality differences and counselling for several major organisations such as the BBC, British Rail, the City of London and Warwick University.

Carol Parkes is a freelance consultant, trainer and coach. She is a medical doctor who specialised in public health medicine and epidemiology. In the past, she has been part of national and international research projects on cancer screening and has many publications in peer-reviewed journals as well as book chapters. She later worked in consultant and leadership roles in the NHS for 10 years before embarking on her current freelance career.

Getting Old

A Positive and Practical
Approach

Rowan Bayne and
Carol Parkes

Routledge
Taylor & Francis Group

LONDON AND NEW YORK

First published 2021
by Routledge
2 Park Square, Milton Park, Abingdon, Oxon OX14 4RN

and by Routledge
605 Third Avenue, New York, NY 10158

Routledge is an imprint of the Taylor & Francis Group, an informa business

British Library Cataloguing-in-Publication Data
A catalogue record for this book is available from the British Library

Library of Congress Cataloging-in-Publication Data
A catalog record for this book has been requested

ISBN: 978-1-138-56601-9 (hbk)
ISBN: 978-1-138-56603-3 (pbk)
ISBN: 978-1-315-12331-8 (ebk)

Always seek the guidance of your doctor or other qualified health
professional with any questions you may have regarding your
health or a medical condition. Never disregard the advice of a
medical professional, or delay in seeking it, because of something
you have read in this book.

The information and suggestions in this book are safe and
accurate to the best of the authors' knowledge. The authors
and publisher do not accept any responsibility for losses that
arise from applying them and we recommend that readers check
their use of them with an appropriately qualified health or other
professional first.

Typeset in Sabon
by Apex CoVantage, LLC

Contents

Acknowledgements

Rowan would like to thank Katherine Bayne for her calm efficiency throughout the writing of this book. Carol would like to thank Jannie Mead for her support and encouragement. And we both appreciated the experience and understanding of the Routledge editorial staff, especially Lucy Kennedy, Helen Pritt and Lottie Mapp.

Introduction

We've written this book for general readers who are feeling interested, worried or shocked about a change or problem in themselves or in someone they care about which could be related to getting old. You also want to do something about such changes, and our central focus is to suggest a variety of practical possibilities for action.

The book is in two main parts. In Section 1, we discuss some core physical and mental aspects of getting old, for example maintaining and increasing mobility, improving sleep and digestion, and becoming a more active participant in consultations with health professionals. In Section 2, we turn to social and psychological aspects of getting old such as choosing where to live, becoming more oneself and using the idea of styles of romantic love.

There is a bleak view of the truth about getting old and a positive one. The bleak view is that as we get old, we get stiffer, more bent over, more achy, incontinent, falling and forgetting more and more and believing that life is all downhill from now on. The positive view is that many older people become stronger through life experience, for example more able to see problems in perspective and more assertive in expressing their emotions and wishes, but this positive view tends to be neglected.

An unusual aspect of the book is its application of personality theory to some of the changes and problems associated with getting old. Thus, in some of the exercises we encourage readers to reflect on what might work for them as a person with their personality traits, motives, strengths and values. In this respect and others, the book recognises that there is truth in the positive view of getting old as well as the bleak one and that there are many practical things we can do to make the last part of our lives healthier and more enjoyable.

Rowan Bayne and Carol Parkes

Physical and mental aspects of getting old

Chapter 1

Mobility

Think of physical changes associated with getting old. For example, you may find that becoming less agile and more doddery are prominent and that negative changes like these come to mind most easily. Moreover, the fact that many of these changes can be slowed or reversed by physical exercise is not exactly welcome to many of us. Accordingly, we begin this chapter with some general principles which attempt to counter this dislike.

1   We define physical exercise very broadly, indeed to mean all physical movement, ranging from a gentle stretch at one extreme to an ultra-marathon at the other. Either of these and anything between can slow or reverse the undesirable physical changes associated with getting old.
2   Exercise should feel good and not be a strain.
3   If you choose to increase the amount or the intensity of an exercise, that too should feel good. If it doesn't, we want you to stop. Generally, this means *gradually* increasing its level, speed, frequency or number.
4   We strongly recommend frequent recovery and rest days. Feeling very tired and aching muscles are useful warning signs, and we want you to listen to your body when deciding how much rest to take, although two recovery days a week may be a helpful general guide. Moreover, injury is more likely in old age, and recovery from injury tends to take longer, so it is much better to prevent it in the first place. It is a myth that lots of pain and effort are required for most of us to make useful improvements in physical fitness.
5   Maintaining or increasing mobility is central to coping with physical ageing for several reasons. First, it reduces the chances of many major illnesses such as heart disease and dementia.

Second, it improves quality of life, for example making falls less likely and positive social contact more likely. Third, it can lead to feeling more alive.

In the rest of this section, we suggest some options for working on muscles, bones, feet, knees and hips, backs, necks, balance, sitting, walking and running.

Muscles, bones, feet etc.

Muscles

Muscles tend to weaken after 30 years old and especially after 70. Moving in any way helps counteract this deterioration, but there are also some exercises which are particularly effective. We outline these and hope you will try one or more of them.

The idea here, consistent with the general principles at the start of this chapter, is to start with an exercise and a level you can do comfortably. Check with your GP or another appropriately qualified health professional that you're not being too enthusiastic in your choice. Ideally, a further safety precaution is for somebody else to be present who is trained in manual handling, and who is fit, alert and strong enough to break your fall if needed. Alternatively, have a sturdy table or worktop in easy grasping distance.

Press-ups: five levels of ease/difficulty

Next we describe several variations of the press-up, ranging from one for beginners to the excruciatingly hard for almost anyone. We don't see the aim as being able to do the excruciatingly difficult variations! (Cf. general principles 2, 3 and 4).

Level 1 press-up

Stand facing a wall, raise your arms and press your palms against the wall and then move your chest towards the wall and back. Do as many press-ups as you can comfortably do and then stop.

Level 2 press-up

Stand next to a sturdy table or worktop, palms on the surface, and bend your knees, pressing down with your hands. Continue until your arm muscles are tired, counting the number of times you can bend and straighten.

Level 3 press-up

Kneeling on the floor, lower your chest towards the floor. Do this once and see how comfortable it feels. If it's not comfortable, go back to level 2.

Level 4: the standard press-up

NB: This level is quite enough for most people.

Lie straight on the floor face down, supported only by your palms (which are placed beneath your shoulders) and by your toes.

Lower your body, breathing out and keeping your body straight and your buttocks squeezed together (imagine clenching a sheet of paper between them).

Lower your chest as close to the floor as is comfortable, breathing out as you do so.

Raise your body using your arms and knees, breathing in as you do it.

That's one standard press-up. Aim to increase the number you do when and if you're ready, bearing the general principles firmly in mind.

Advanced press-ups

There are lots of variations, e.g. holding one leg in the air, clapping hands between press ups, or resting both feet on a bench with your hands on the floor or ground.

Squats: two levels of ease/difficulty

Like press-ups, squats are a weight-bearing exercise, widely used and effective. They are more practical for some of us than press-ups.

Level 1: beginners' squat

Sit on the edge of a firm chair, hands clasped in front of your chest, and stand. Keep your weight on your heels.

Sit on the edge of the chair and repeat when and if your body feels ready.

As before, count the number you feel comfortable with and aim to increase it and/or your speed.

Level 2: the standard squat

Start standing, with your hands in front, feet shoulder width apart and squat as if to sit on a chair.

Other exercises for the main muscles include walking and running (discussed later in this chapter), weight-lifting and going up steps or stairs.

Also, we suggest eating some protein and carbohydrates in the hour or so after exercise and remembering to rest and recover.

Bones

Bones tend to become less dense and therefore weaker in old age. The main causes of this are not enough calcium and vitamin D, so eating dairy foods and protein, and getting plenty of sunshine, can be helpful. Even standing helps maintain calcium levels a little. However, bone is living tissue and needs stimulating through feedback and, in particular, impacts of the kind produced by jumping, running and dancing – but not cycling and swimming, because although good for cardiovascular health, they are not weight-bearing.

Feet

The health of young feet is often taken for granted. In contrast, old feet are prone to several problems, for example dry skin forming corns, thickening toenails (to the extent that they can't be cut in the usual way) and fungus infections (which if left untreated become very unsightly). Such changes can limit mobility, the first making movement painful, the other two through feeling embarrassed.

Having corns removed by a competent chiropodist is painless and the results are a pleasure. As a friend said after his first visit (in his mid-70s): 'It's like having two new feet'.

Thick toenails are easily trimmed by a chiropodist. Fungus infections take much longer because toenails grow slowly and the many remedies prominent in chemists are, in the experience of one of us and his chiropodist, not very effective (they may well recommend a liquid medicine). Treatment with a laser is potentially much quicker but much more expensive, and the evidence for its effectiveness is unclear so far. Washing socks at 60 degrees and spraying anti-fungal spray inside shoes are also part of the treatment.

There are some basic exercises for increasing foot core stability – they focus on a set of muscles that affect many other aspects and parts of our bodies including backs and posture, but tend to be neglected. You may like to try the following daily:

> Sitting on a firm chair, place your bare feet flat on a towel. Wriggle your toes, then seize the towel with them and scrunch it towards you. Try for a minute or two twice a day.
>
> Sitting on the floor or a chair, 'write' the alphabet with your toes one foot at a time.

Knees and hips

Pain in knees and hips can be caused in several ways and may be diagnosed wrongly as just 'part of getting old' or as needing surgery when they don't. The causes include obesity and muscle imbalance and overuse, and the treatment options, apart from an operation, are medication, losing weight and structured exercises supervised by a physiotherapist. Generally, and obviously, it is best to try simpler procedures first.

If you do decide to have an operation to replace a joint, we suggest asking your GP which surgeons they and other GPs would go to for that operation themselves.

Ways of keeping joints healthy are regular exercise (with recovery and rest days), avoiding too much twisting, kneeling or lifting, and only occasional or no sugary food or drink (because they may cause inflammation).

Lower backs

For lower back pain, continue with normal activities as far as possible and vary the position of your body. It is a myth that the best treatment is bed rest or lying on the floor, although this was for many years the standard treatment, sometimes for several months, when the result of just a couple of days in bed is weaker muscles and bones and a slightly increased risk of dying from a blood clot.

The following exercises are worth considering for lower back pain:

- squats (see earlier in this chapter)
- brisk walking, arms swinging, head up (if it hurts, go more slowly for a while or stop)
- deep breathing in a relaxed way and using your diaphragm (rest your hands on your stomach and make it swell with your breath)
- mindfulness (deep breathing may be the active ingredient)
- whole body exercises, like running, dancing and swimming
- yoga, Pilates and the gym suit some people and not others – too much twisting and bending for them

Back pain is thus not inevitable with ageing, and we can do several things to help prevent it: being active (as discussed later in this chapter), maintaining a healthy weight (see the section on Diet in Chapter 2), eating and drinking well (both discussed in Chapter 2) and choosing a bed that suits you.

There is no such thing as an orthopaedic bed or mattress. Appealing as the idea may be, it is just a marketing term. A bed needs to be comfortable for you – e.g. you should not feel that the mattress is swallowing you, nor should it feel like a board – and it is probably worth changing a mattress after a few years. We also recommend the back stretcher developed by Neil Summers, especially after a warm bath, for a few minutes at a time.

Overall, drugs (including pain killers), surgery and injections are much more risky ways of treating back pain and are often useless. The simplest and (as it happens) the cheapest options are the most generally effective and safe, and most back pain heals itself. For the latest guidance, see nice.org.uk.

Necks

Neck pain is common and not usually a sign of serious illness, though it is of course painful and awkward. Possible exercises to try, very gently, are 1) stretch your neck, stopping if it hurts, by pointing your nose at the ceiling and moving it from side to side, 2) move your head from side to side, looking over each shoulder and using your hands to stretch a little further, and 3) put your chin on your chest. If these exercises don't work, see a physiotherapist.

Falls and balance

Falls are both more likely and more dangerous for older people. Broken bones can mean months of pain and anxiety, and loss of mobility and independence.

The risk of falling increases at around 65 years old. This is because we have far fewer of the nerve cells which specialise in balance and coordination by then. Moreover, this loss is true for athletes as well as the general population: general fitness doesn't prevent it, but particular exercises like those outlined next do.

Injuries from falls can be reduced and prevented by doing some of the following:

- press-ups (see earlier in this chapter) to strengthen wrists and arms, thus absorbing much of the impact of most falls and making your head less likely to hit the ground
- squats (see earlier in this chapter) to strengthen legs and prevent or reduce falling in the first place

Be especially careful with the following exercises: start them holding onto, or next to, something sturdy to steady yourself if you lose your balance – a wall or a table, but not a person.

- Stand on one leg when doing everyday things such as watching TV. How many seconds can you stand without wobbling? A much more difficult variation is to close your eyes before you lift one of your feet, and keep your eyes closed. As before, the aim is to do this comfortably and without wobbling.

Generally we think it better to compete with yourself, for example in how long you can stand on one leg, but you may prefer to compete with the average score of others or with a judgement on what is a 'good score' for your age group (or a younger one). For the standing on one leg exercise with eyes open, 20 or 30 seconds is a good score for people in their 70s. In marked contrast, young adults can generally stand on one leg with their eyes closed for 30 seconds or more.

Some hospitals run clinics on improving balance using these and other exercises. Also, falls can be made less likely by being a healthy weight, checking your home for objects that could trip you up, looking after your feet, hearing and eyesight, reviewing your medication with a chemist or GP and considering aids such as handrails and walking sticks.

Pilates, tai chi and yoga are also very effective for improving some people's balance, and karate teaches ways of falling more safely.

Anyone concerned about having a higher risk of falling or a recent fall should speak to their doctor. Health professionals are trained to take a preventive approach to managing falls, and there are useful guidelines developed by NICE on this (which are being updated as new evidence on prevention and treatment of falls has emerged).

A comprehensive assessment of fall risk can be carried out, and specific treatments or interventions will be recommended. These focus on associated health problems and also relevant issues in the home environment.

Exercise (defined broadly)

In this section, we discuss sitting and walking, the latter being a very beneficial exercise for most of us and the former surprisingly unhealthy (as has been realised only recently). We also, for those who wish to go further than walking, describe High Intensity Interval Training (HIIT) and some ideas about links between personality and choice of exercise.

Sitting

Long periods of sitting contribute to lower back and neck pain, hips and hamstrings that are too tight, weak core muscles, being overweight and a greater risk of serious illnesses such as type 2 diabetes, some forms of cancer and strokes. Several causes of such effects have been identified or proposed, for example, raised blood pressure, shallow breathing, less breaking down of fat and sugar in the blood stream and arteries becoming stiffer.

It feels rather eerie to think of all these processes happening as we do an apparently harmless thing like sitting down. Moreover, they happen however much exercise you do at other times. Essentially, we are a lot more healthy when we're moving enough (and also taking appropriate amounts of rest and relaxation).

Some options to counter the damaging effects of sitting are:

- two minutes standing for every 20 or so minutes of sitting, but with care, especially if you have lower back or circulation problems
- two minutes walking during each hour of sitting

- breathing more deeply
- squats (again!)
- fidgeting

Overall, gradually integrate more moving and kinds of moving into your daily life. There are many opportunities to move more and increase strength and flexibility at the same time. And remember enjoyment and rest too.

Walking

Walking, either strolling or walking briskly, aids mobility and is good for several parts of our bodies, especially bones, hearts and, perhaps surprisingly, brains – both cognitive performance and mood are positively affected. Walking is also aerobic, generally free of side effects, easy on hips, ankles and knees, not expensive and easily integrated into everyday life for most of us.

A mixture of jogging and walking, slow jogging and faster jogging are further options and get closer to a very effective form of exercise called High Intensity Interval Training (HIIT).

High Intensity Interval Training (HIIT)

In HIIT, 'high intensity' is doing something physical, e.g. lifting weights, walking, running, swimming or cycling for as hard and long as you comfortably can. 'Interval' refers to the recovery time between each intense period. For example, one person might do three sprints of 20 seconds each for the Intensity element, with intervals at a gentle pace and about three minutes long (and perhaps downhill) between each one. Alternatively, in some research the intervals have lasted for as long as it takes for the participants' pulse rates to drop below 120.

If you decide to try HIIT yourself, please read the following further information and advice before doing so and apply the general principles at the start of this chapter too.

A refinement in some research has been to start with several weeks of preparation designed especially for those who haven't exercised for a while. For example, the participants walk 10 minutes a day for the first week, gradually increasing over the next four weeks and then adding brisker walking etc. until ready for HIIT itself. The participants in some of the studies have been in their 60s and 70s.

The results of a few weeks of HIIT include, for example, lower blood pressure and blood glucose, reduced fat, and increased leg strength and aerobic fitness. Overall, HIIT's method of shorter, harder and fewer sessions plus recovery time is very effective. The striking aspects are just how short the sessions are (and generally they are for one, two or three sessions a week) and how much effect they have. The studies have been carried out on many groups of people, including some with diabetes or recovering from recent heart attacks.

A specific example of one person's HIIT is to warm up on an exercise bike for two minutes, then gradually speed up and increase the resistance on the bike at the same time until he ends this phase with 20 seconds going flat out. He then cycles gently for long enough to feel ready for another sprint of 20 seconds then another minute or so of gentle cycling and a final all-out 20 seconds.

However, please note that he has been doing HIIT for some time and it is very important to ease your way in and also to consult an appropriate health professional first.

A reaction against 'pure HIIT' called Liss may appeal more. Liss stands for Low Intensity Steady State Cardio and is continuous exercise at a much slower pace for 30 to 60 minutes. The principle of gradually increasing the amount applies to Liss too. An attractive variation for some people is to do HIIT, Liss and rest days, each of them on different days.

Personality and exercise

Different kinds of exercise seem likely to suit people with different personalities. Suzanne Brue uses a colour system, and there is a brief quiz to indicate which colour represents your personality in this sense at www.the8colors.com. For example, people who are whites in her model tend to enjoy exercising alone in a calm, familiar and pleasing setting and letting their minds drift – exercise as a 'moving meditation' – whereas reds tend to want lots of stimulation, variety and quick responding – exercise as absorbing action. Thus, motives may be the key to finding the form of exercise which suits you. (See the section in Chapter 7 on personality development for more on the personality theory used by Brue.)

Chapter 2

Diet and digestion

Diet

It is no surprise that many people are confused about what constitutes a healthy diet. The 'official' advice changes over the decades, and the truth about what we should and shouldn't eat is often debunked as new evidence emerges. It is tempting, therefore, to give up on listening to advice and just eat whatever you fancy. This would be a mistake, and it is particularly important to eat as healthy a diet as possible as we age.

There are two main problems with diet research and advice. The first is that eating is such a deeply personal thing that we do for all sorts of reasons, not just hunger. We may do it for emotional reasons, habit, culture, beliefs, finances, availability, etc. It is therefore difficult to do good research on it as people often can't really remember what they eat, or miscalculate it – and people don't like to be dictated to in order to stick to a certain diet that can be followed up on in a research study. It is a lot easier to study rats in lab cages than it is free-range humans. It was much easier to do the research on the link between smoking and health than diet and health because smoking is a much more categorical, concrete thing to know about and recall or stick to. People can more easily say whether they have smoked 20 cigarettes a day for the last week than recall their diet in a retrospective study or stick to a diet regime in a prospective study.

The second problem is that diet is political. There is big money to be made from certain components of food, and some countries rely heavily on the economic proceeds of these. For example, there is a big business in the USA in producing relatively cheap corn, and so products of this industry, like high fructose corn syrup (HFCS), have been pushed into human food. If you add natural human taste preferences for, say, sweetness, and a money maker like corn, then the two combine into a perfect marriage. But it is not necessarily a healthy union – the human cost can be obesity and other sugar-related problems.

There are a dazzling number of books and articles on diet, and it would be a full-time job to read them all. Many have completely opposing messages. Diet is one area where all sorts of people have their own theories and advice, and in the age of social media, this can be very confusing. British doctor Tim Spector spent five years drawing on his medical, genetics and epidemiological skills to produce an excellent overview of the science and epidemiology behind diet (*The Diet Myth*, published in 2015). He examines not just what is a healthy diet but also what is it that has made too many people overweight or obese in recent decades.

He points out that people are different in all sorts of ways and one size doesn't necessarily fit all. Studying identical twins is a great way of teasing out what differences are due to genetics. He found that 60–70% of differences in responses to diet were genetic, i.e. contributing to the degree to which people are likely to put on weight, their food preferences and even their liking for exercise.

He thinks that looking at diet in just its component micronutrient parts (protein, fat, carbohydrates etc.) is far too simple. One of the largest influences on diet and health never appears on the food labels. It is trillions of microbes that live in us and in particular in our guts. We become colonised with bacteria from our mother when we are born (vaginally) and, despite modern obsessions with antiseptic 'cleanliness', the majority of these bacteria that live in and on us are friendly and health-giving. The whole community of microbes (mainly bacteria) in our gut is referred to as our microbiome. It is now thought that decreasing the diversity and amount of microbiome (from our diet and lifestyle) is a large factor in explaining the current epidemic of obesity. Lack of diversity in our diets and the high consumption of processed foods that contain mainly corn, soy, wheat and meat have depleted our microbiome.

It is not just food that affects our microbiome; it is also how much exercise we do. The fitter we are physically, the fitter our gut microbiome is. It has been shown that is better to be fat yet fit rather than thin and unfit in terms of reducing heart disease and overall mortality.

Antibiotics, though of course useful and sometimes life-saving, can dramatically reduce the numbers and diversity of good bacteria, but a healthy diet can restore them quite quickly.

So what do we eat as we get older? In terms of what is sensible for most people (of any age) to eat, there is now reasonably good evidence from lots of studies that are pulled together into large meta-analyses. The following are pointers:

1   Avoid processed foods as much as possible. This pretty much means anything that your great grandparents didn't eat and anything that wasn't picked, dug up, harvested or obtained directly from an animal. Processed foods taste good to a lot of people because they usually have a carefully calculated combination of fat, sugar and salt – and many people find this combo irresistible, and our brains can get very accustomed to this heady, pleasure-giving mix. They are also good for the food industry as filling food with these can extend their transportation and distribution times and shelf life.

2   Too much sugar is not good for us, and we should be very careful how much we are eating without realising it. It is an ingredient of many things that aren't that obviously 'sweet', like soups – as well as many processed foods, already mentioned. When people became scared of fats in foods from the 'low-fat movement' in the 1980s onwards, it allowed the food industry to up the sugar levels instead to keep things tasting okay. It has been estimated that our sugar consumption has been increasing at about 10% each decade since 1990, and we are eating about 20 times more than our great grandparents did. Liquid sugar can increase sugar consumption considerably, so it is wise to avoid sugary drinks and be aware that a lot of fruit juices and smoothies are packed full of sugar. Although twin studies have shown that having a sweet tooth is about 50% genetic, we still need to actively work on decreasing our actual sugar consumption and wean ourselves off the high sugar taste.

3   Reduce your intake of red meat, especially processed meats like sausages, ham and salami. This can help decrease risks of dying early. Non-processed poultry meat is a healthier option for meat eaters. There are fewer studies on fish eating, but it is unlikely to be harmful. Of course, there are other reasons for people to cut down on meat eating – environmental reasons and wanting to avoid antibiotics and hormones in some non-organic meats.

4   Increase your consumption of fresh vegetables and fruit – sticking to the five-portions-a-day recommendation is sensible. Examples of a portion are a small apple, six medium-size

strawberries and three heads of broccoli. The Mediterranean-style diet has been repeatedly shown to be healthy and reduces the rate of disease (such as heart attacks and stroke) and death rates. This involves eating a lot of whole grains, legumes and vegetables, nuts and fruits. The diet uses plenty of olive oil (containing mono-unsaturated fatty acids), which has been shown to be healthy, demonstrating that earlier decades' preoccupation with low-fat diets was misdirected. The diet incorporates moderate amounts of fish, poultry, yogurt and cheese, but less red meat and processed meat. Moderate amounts of red wine can be consumed with meals.

5   If you can keep to low to moderate amounts, then coffee, red wine and dark chocolate are likely to be okay for most people as they haven't been shown to have negative health effects. However, for some people who find it difficult to restrict their consumption, it may be easier to have none rather than risk bingeing.

A healthy weight

Most people gain weight with age, and it is often seen as a natural part of getting old. However, it isn't inevitable, and it is a major threat to health.

A straightforward, low-tech and sufficiently precise way of measuring healthy and unhealthy amounts of weight is to measure your waist. This method allows for muscle being heavier than fat, which can result in people with well-developed muscles being wrongly rated as overweight. Moreover, fat stored around the waist is the most dangerous for health: too much fat in this area substantially increases the risks of several types of cancer, high blood pressure, osteoarthritis and type 2 diabetes.

To measure your waist, put a tape measure around the middle of your waist, usually at the navel. Stay comfortably relaxed – tightening your stomach muscles is cheating! How much you've recently eaten or drunk will make a difference, but great precision is not needed. A waist measure of more than 32" (81cm) in women and more than 37" (94cm) in men is usually interpreted as too much. Another way of interpreting a waist measurement is that it's healthy when it's less than half a person's height without shoes. However, for both ways of measuring there's also a cautionary note for people who are slim: some of us are slim outside but have hidden fat inside. Unfortunately, discovering this requires a scan.

Losing weight

You may wish to lose weight. If so, the standard advice used to be to 'eat less and exercise more'. This advice implies that losing weight is just a matter of will power and discipline, which is a myth and much too simple and unfair. As already mentioned, about 70% of our propensity to put on weight is genetic, and unfortunately, these genes tend to overlap with genes that make us less inclined to do exercise, so it is a double whammy. However, that doesn't mean we have no influence on our weight, as we are not predestined to be overweight. It may mean that some people have to work harder at it than others and need to be very aware of all the factors that are involved in becoming overweight. They include diet, the microbiome, exercise, habits and how we eat, medication, mini-fasting and personality.

Diet

The previous sections on diet gave guidance on what dietary habits are healthy and more likely to keep you at a healthy weight. Reducing our consumption of processed food and refined sugar will be a mainstay in weight reduction. To make it possible to adhere to new habits, they need to be enjoyable and motivating.

The microbiome

Looking after our microbiome is a vital part of losing weight – we need to make sure we eat a diverse and varied diet to tend our microbiome. All of the previous diet pointers will have a positive effect on the microbiome.

Exercise

It is ironic that eating less can result in feeling less energetic, thus using less calories, and that lots of exercise can make us hungrier. Added to this, it has been found that just increasing exercise in order to lose weight is unlikely to work – the body compensates and slows its metabolism down in order to stop breaking down fat. It needs to be a combination of both diet and exercise that does the trick. Although exercise alone may not be great at shifting the weight, it is beneficial for all sorts of other reasons. Doing no exercise at all is twice as risky as being obese in terms of dying early.

The risk of heart disease is higher if you are a person who smokes and doesn't eat vegetables than if you are a non-smoking, vegetable-eating, fit, obese person. Another major good thing about exercise is that it affects your microbiome – it grows larger and becomes more diverse, which has many health benefits, as mentioned earlier.

Habits and how we eat

Eating too quickly can cause us to overeat (it takes about 20 minutes from starting eating to the brain reacting with sensations of not being hungry). One of the difficult things about eating sugary food is that we don't have a natural 'that's enough button' in our bodies and we can easily gorge on it. It is much more difficult to do that with foods containing predominantly fat or protein – we tend to know that we have had enough and stop more easily.

There are many ways in which we can develop healthier eating habits that will help us not to overeat or eat the wrong things. Examples are the oft-quoted 'don't go food shopping when you are hungry', shopping from a list and not having certain things in the house if you know you can't resist them. Actual eating habits are important, like taking time over meals (like many Mediterranean people do) and chewing properly.

Medication

A side effect of some medications is to increase appetite and to put on weight. If your doctor prescribes one of these on an ongoing basis, it is worth discussing how you will manage your weight at the same time and plan it pro-actively rather than deal with it later once the weight is on. A compensatory change in diet and exercise may be required to keep your weight more stable.

Mini-fasting

There are several variations of mini-fasts, including the widely publicised 5:2 diet, which is five days a week eating whatever you want and the other two non-consecutive days restricting yourself to 600 calories for a man and 500 for a woman.

A variation is the alternate days diet, which assumes that bodies respond well to routine. In this diet, the 'fast' is again relative: about 500 calories, usually eaten as one meal. The research on this approach shows clearly that health improves and weight reduces. Another benefit was that participants 'rediscovered hunger', felt it to be quite different from just being hungry, and liked the feeling.

Mini-fasting is very simple and flexible. It combines being gentle and tough, self-indulgent and disciplined (but not for long). A mini-fast day can be not eating from, say, after lunch to the same time the next day or from 5pm to 7 the next morning. On 'feast' days, you can eat anything, though obviously some foods contribute less to losing weight.

A further benefit is that the mini-fast approach gives your metabolism a rest and time for repairs. In this respect, it is like vigorous exercise: interspersing deliberate stress and recovery periods and treating both as important.

Check with your GP or other appropriate health professional if you're thinking of trying any kind of fast. Two useful general principles are to make changes gradually and to monitor your reactions carefully and preferably with someone else involved too. Other limitations of fasting are that the long-term effects of the different variations are not yet known, that side effects like dizziness and headaches occur in a few people and that it is not recommended for children, women in pregnancy or for people with eating disorders or type 1 diabetes.

In addition, the mini-fast approach implies that a number of established ideas about losing weight are myths, e.g. that eating breakfast is a useful, even major, part of successfully losing weight, and that grazing – eating little and often – is healthy, which is a myth despite its attractive rationale of maintaining a stable blood sugar level and being a natural way of eating. However, it may be that grazing suits some people and mini-fasting suits others: back to trial and error to find out what works for you, but with the added factor of personality to take into account.

Personality and eating less

The underlying principle and assumption here is that if your strategy for eating less fits your personality, it will be more likely to work. For example, a major personality difference is that some people like and indeed need plans and routine more than they like keeping things flexible and open, while others have exactly the opposite priority. Calorie counting is seen as more likely to work with people with the first personality characteristic. However, we can sometimes benefit from adding a *little* of the approach opposite to our own: mini-fasting when the mood takes you can work better with some discipline, and sticking to a plan can work better with some flexibility.

For example, X hated herself for being overweight, and her GP attributed her non-compliance to numerous standard techniques, like calorie counting and keeping a diary of what she ate, as an effect of her core personality and therefore that she was very unlikely to change. Another GP was more optimistic. He took a more positive interpretation of X's personality and saw her as strongly resenting rules and plans and therefore more likely to respond well to a 'sort of' diet. This means lots of variety and flexibility, therefore stocking up with healthy and mainly low-calorie food and enjoying choosing just before eating while trying to eat a bit less than usual. It also means not keeping many high-calorie foods within easy reach, because X and people of her temperament tend to have poor impulse control (but good mental flexibility).

The different strategies are each more likely to work with people of one of four personality temperaments (see the sections on personality and core motives in Chapter 7). The strategies are summarised here. They also suggest which strategies are likely to be futile or counterproductive for each temperament.

The four temperaments and their implications for losing weight are:

1   Using or developing their natural strength of being in touch with feeling hungry and with when they are full. Refine this to judging what *exactly* it is that they want to eat. Also, make dieting as much fun as possible, and don't plan. Focus on the process, not on goals.
2   Planning meals and times. Use their natural strengths of being strong-willed, organised and task-focused.
3   Liking to know theory and to design their own variations of diets. Want reasons and evidence.
4   Needing to find a personal meaning for losing weight, such as doing it for someone else. Will diet when it feels right, and are likely to diet in bursts.

Some problems with bladders and bowels

Bladders

Bladders become less elastic as we get older. They hold less urine, and urination becomes more frequent and less efficient with more chance of the bladder not being fully emptied and an increased chance of leakage and incontinence. Getting up once a night to pee is regarded as a normal part of getting old, twice is border-line, while about every three to four hours is a typical healthy frequency during the day. Drinking less as a self-treatment is very tempting but a bad idea, because it can lead to dehydration.

Dehydration

Dehydration is not drinking enough fluids to be healthy, which ironically is sometimes the result of trying to reduce episodes of incontinence or frequency of urinating, particularly at night. Other causes are not being able to feel thirsty and not enough fluids being available. Older people sometimes decrease the amount they drink until only drinking, say, two cups of tea a day. The possible consequences include increased drowsiness (which can be mistaken for the normal process of dying described in Chapter 10), headaches, skin and eye problems, confusion (can be mistaken for dementia), urinary infections, crystals and kidney failure.

Two indicators that you are drinking enough fluid are the colour of your urine – ideally colourless or pale yellow – and a moist mouth. Another is of course feeling thirsty, but some of us have lost this ability or misinterpret it as tiredness or hunger.

The question of how much fluid is healthy is controversial, with eight glasses of water a day winning the publicity battle for many years. At the level of individual needs, several factors such as weight and amount of sweating are relevant, but generally around one to two litres a day for men and one to one-and-a-half for women is probably optimal. However, individual differences in physical and biochemical characteristics are usually substantial, and we suggest experimenting to find what suits you. Our bodies are usually adept at monitoring how much fluid we need.

Incontinence

Both urinary and faecal incontinence can usually be cured or managed, but diagnoses of the causes can be complicated. Common causes of urinary incontinence are enlarged prostate glands, overactive bladders, urinary infections, other illnesses such as diabetes and cysts. Common causes of faecal incontinence are poor mobility, constipation, diarrhoea, lack of fibre, lack of fluids and certain drugs.

Your GP may offer diagnoses and treatments, or you can ask them to refer you to a continence service or centre. Self-referral is often available too. There are NHS specialist services in most areas of the UK. Just put 'continence service' plus the nearest town or county into Google.

Typical help with and treatments of urinary incontinence include continence pads, penile sheaths, avoiding certain drinks and foods (because they irritate some bladders; examples are coffee, tea, alcohol and curries), exercises for pelvic floors and bladder retraining. Several drugs are also used, for example to relax relevant muscles.

Some of the procedures and treatments involve a risk-benefits judgement, and one, vaginal mesh, has been banned by the NHS because of severe problems with it. Others are completely safe. For example, one approach to understanding your bladder is to keep a diary for a few days and nights listing 1) what you drink, how much and when and 2) how much you urinate and when.

Two exercises for strengthening pelvic floor muscles (summarised from Marion Shoard's book *How To Handle Later Life*) are:

Breathe normally throughout the following two exercises. The first exercise is to gently but firmly tense the muscles that you'd use if you wanted to stop urinating and excreting faeces – these are the pelvic floor muscles. Hold each contraction for as long as you comfortably can, rest for a few seconds and repeat up to 10 times. Try to avoid tightening muscles in your abdomen and buttocks. A second exercise is to tighten the pelvic floor muscles quickly and then at once let them go. Pause for a second, and repeat until the muscles are tired.

Some authorities consider pelvic floor exercises to be straightforward; others see them as simple ideas but risky if they're done incorrectly. We recommend checking your technique with your GP or continence nurse. Also, a lot of patience may be needed – a few months of doing the exercises before they have an effect is quite normal.

Bladder retraining

Retraining your bladder to 'hold on' for two hours is a realistic aim. (Young bladders are typically elastic enough to manage four hours comfortably.) The training involves a gradual increase in the length of times between the first sign of wanting to urinate and doing it – for example, perhaps 10 minutes holding on during the first week, then 15 minutes the next week and so on. Techniques that help in holding on include distraction (sitting on a firm chair, music, going through the alphabet thinking of first names which begin with each letter) and contracting your pelvic floor muscles.

Catheters versus incontinence pads

In her 2017 book *How to Handle Later Life*, Marion Shoard argues strongly against the use of urinary catheters in normal practice. Her main reasons are that catheters are a significant source of urinary infections (which can be very serious) and that they can interfere with the ability of bladders to return to functioning normally after treatment. In contrast, incontinence pads don't cause infections if they are changed often enough and don't interfere with restoring normal functioning. They are also now available in a wide range of sizes and shapes and can cope well with much larger quantities of urine than used to be the case. Shoard quotes from Royal College of Nursing guidelines, which state: 'Never catheterise or continue catheter usage for nursing convenience'.

Bowels

Normal bowel movements vary considerably from one person to another in frequency – from three times a day to once every three days – but they should be comfortable to do, fairly firm and not a strain. You may find the idea of not more than 80% effort as a desirable maximum useful here.

The best position for bowel movements is described and strongly recommended by Giulia Enders in her book *Gut, the Inside Story of Our Body's Most Under-rated Organ*. She calls this position 'squatting while sitting', and it makes constipation, piles and diverticulitis less likely by relaxing the relevant muscles and straightening the part of our digestive system which leads into the anus.

To squat while sitting on a toilet, you lean forward slightly and either put your feet on a low footstool or achieve the same effect by raising your heels. A variation recommended by Enders for treating persistent constipation is the 'rocking squat' – sitting on the toilet, bend your upper body forward, then straighten, and repeat a few times.

Constipation

Constipation means straining to pass stools or doing so less frequently than is usual for you without another explanation, e.g. eating less. A change in frequency that persists may indicate a health problem.

Drinking more and eating more fibre usually cures constipation: we recommend increasing the amount of fibre you eat by small amounts, and slowly! It is possible to experiment too enthusiastically with, for example, bran, become 'blocked', and need to see your GP. Allow about 36 hours between an increase of fibre and any effects.

Other sources of high fibre include flaxseed, wholemeal flour and pulses and fruit and vegetables generally. Michael Mosley in his book *Clever Guts* recommends seaweed capsules.

Chapter 3

Sleep

Poor-quality sleep contributes to accidents, bad decisions, illness, etc. If you're not sleeping well, you may wish to experiment with some of the suggestions in this chapter.

As a guideline to a desirable amount of sleep, there is general agreement that most people need seven to nine hours' good-quality sleep a night, but with wide individual variation. Feeling awake during most of most days is a good sign that you sleep well enough, and this is the case however much you experience your sleep as fitful and broken. Conversely, daytime tiredness can be caused by factors other than not sleeping well.

Improving your sleep

Advice on improving sleep is readily available, e.g. at www.rcpsych. ac.uk and www.raysahelian.com/sleep. Small changes to diet, bedroom environment, etc. can be very effective. In this section, we suggest some other options for improving sleep quality and quantity, some chosen as most likely to work generally, others as more unusual and not widely known about. The approach is one of trial and error, testing one change or technique at a time for several days. They are an eclectic mix of options, some of which work for some people. If you give them a fair chance and they don't work, your GP or other health professionals will have other suggestions, principally counselling and medication. Sleeping pills should be taken for very short periods if at all because of the risk of dependence, the difficulty for some people of withdrawal and the sleep the pills induce not being as healthy as natural sleep.

Insomnia is used as a general term for sleep difficulties, and like others comes in varying degrees of seriousness ranging from disabling to quite readily responding to relatively simple treatment. The following suggestions for improving sleep quality are for you to consider trying yourself. The first method is a general review or audit which may lead to specific changes to try out. The others are examples of such changes.

• Audit all the aspects of your life which may be affecting your sleep. These may include where you sleep, e.g. how dark it is, quality of mattress and pillows, how well or not you fit with someone you sleep with, noise, temperature, how you prepare (if you do) to go to sleep or to go to bed and so on. Reviewing these aspects of your life can in itself be a powerful step to improving your sleep.
• Reduce the amount of caffeine you drink (for some people caffeine has no effect at all on sleep, whatever time of day or night they drink it, while others are very sensitive).
• What do you do in the hour or so before bed? It may be worth trying a more relaxing routine than your usual, or creating a routine if you don't have one at all. Bodies and minds, or at least some of them, prepare themselves for sleep both through relaxation and the familiarity of a routine. They like to know what's coming. Other minds and bodies thrive on not knowing.
• People who usually fall asleep easily don't try to do it; it just happens (alright for some!). One way of trying to do what they do is to concentrate on what's going on in your mind and body: thoughts, feelings, sensations.
• A variation is trying to stay awake, which may seem paradoxical or perverse, but makes sense as a distraction from trying to go to sleep.
• Get more exercise, but note that the time of day you do it may make a difference.
• Reduce alcohol – it's a sedative which tends to result in shallow, fitful sleep.
• Try a writing exercise. There are many possibilities here, the most effective for people in general being to write a specific and achievable to-do list for the next day. Do this just before settling down to see if you'll sleep (but think of it as resting rather than trying to sleep).
• Dim the house lights for the last hour or so before bed.

Snoring

Some of the main causes of snoring are smoking, drinking alcohol and being overweight. It is linked to heart disease and strokes and can affect sleep quality. Other causes include some medications and old injuries to the nose or jaw. It matters partly because it is dangerous – see the section on sleep apnoea in this chapter. Effective treatments follow from the causes and range from lifestyle changes to surgery by an ENT surgeon.

Night cramps

Night cramps, usually in the legs or feet, are very painful but not usually a sign of illness. To counter them, you might try sleeping with your legs slightly raised; doing calf stretches during the day, before bed and when cramping; doing squats; getting a massage; and adding more magnesium (dark chocolate is a good source) and potassium (e.g. bananas) to your diet.

Sleep disorders

Three sleep disorders – sleep apnoea, restless legs syndrome (RLS) and REM sleep behaviour disorder (RBD) – are discussed next. Accurate diagnosis of sleep disorders may require an overnight stay at a specialist clinic which your GP refers you to. Diagnosis is complicated by the same symptoms occurring in different disorders; for example dream enactments occur in RBD, sleep terrors, Post Traumatic Stress Disorder, sleep apnoea, epilepsy and as a side effect of some drugs or withdrawal from them. These disorders or causes need different treatments.

REM sleep behaviour disorder

In REM sleep behaviour disorder (RBD), the paralysis which usually occurs during dreams is partial or absent, so that the dreamer acts out aspects of their dreams. The movements in dream enactments are typically flailing, kicking and jumping or sometimes diving out of bed. The patient may also talk, shout, scream or wail. Injury to oneself or a bed partner is quite common before diagnosis and successful treatment.

The content of the dreams is quite often characteristic: the patient is defending themselves or playing a heroic role. The dreams thus have a threat at their heart and are often vivid and violent. They are also remembered clearly when the dreamer wakes up and later, unlike most dreams, which fade quickly.

A preliminary diagnosis of RBD can be made by asking, 'Have you ever been told that you act out your dreams?' or to a bed partner, 'Have you ever known X to act out a dream, where acting out means flailing or punching?' A formal diagnosis of RBD requires an overnight stay at a sleep clinic, where lack of muscle paralysis and dreaming states are both monitored. Dream enactment does occur in some other conditions, for example sleep terrors and PTSD, which complicates the diagnosis.

There is currently no cure for RBD, but the symptoms can be managed effectively. First, the bedroom is modified to make it safer. For example, one or more inflatable mattresses can be deployed on their sides or flat between the bed and wall(s), and furniture with sharp edges can be moved away from the bed. Some people use a sleeping bag.

Second, melatonin or clonazepam tablets are taken shortly before going to bed. Clonazepam, a drug related to Valium, used to be the first treatment to try, but debilitating side effects and withdrawal problems are much more likely with it than with melatonin. Both medications work, but some patients respond best to one or the other or, in a few patients, to both simultaneously. Melatonin itself comes in two forms, standard and slow release (Circadin), and again each of these is most effective with different patients. Why they and clonazepam work at all is so far not well understood.

A calm period before sleep is probably helpful. Another non-drug treatment that is plausible but as far as we know has not been tested rigorously is 'lucid dreaming', when the dreamer controls the content of their dream, in this case removing or reducing any threat element.

Restless legs

Restless legs syndrome (RLS) is an intense and overwhelming need to move your legs because of sensations variously described as tingling, aching, burning, etc. It tends to come on while relaxing and disappear when moving, but only very briefly, and to be worse at night. It is much more distressing than the term 'restless' sounds and can be very debilitating both in itself and because it disturbs sleep. It affects 5–10% of the general population and is more common with age.

The causes of RLS are not well understood but are seen as physical rather than psychological, with an imbalance of dopamine (a neurotransmitter) and lesions on the brain stem possible explanations. However, it may be that the same symptoms have different causes in different people, and a wide variety of causes have been suggested, e.g. low levels of iron, dehydration, too much exercise, too little exercise, too much sitting, a side effect of some drugs and some illnesses.

RLS is generally difficult to treat effectively. Apart from walking and the treatments which follow from some of the possible causes listed earlier, sufferers rub, bang and squeeze their legs; stretch their calves and hamstrings; reduce smoking, coffee and alcohol consumption; apply Pernaton gel; cup their hands over their mouths and breathe in and out; and apply hot and cold packs. There are also herbal treatments (which imply circulatory and neurological causes if they work) and drugs. The drugs currently prescribed tend to be needed in increasing doses and to have significant side effects. (See the section on medication in Chapter 5.) Overall, the treatments (alone or combined) do work sometimes, and generally it is of course a matter of cautious trial and error and balancing potential risks and benefits.

Sleep apnoea

Sleep apnoea is the result of snoring that restricts breathing so much that it deprives the snorer of oxygen. He or she stops breathing, splutters or snorts, moves position, stops breathing again and so on.

The causes include sleeping on one's back, a blocked nose, being overweight, smoking, drinking alcohol, an underactive thyroid and sedatives. The effects include daytime sleepiness and heart disease. Diagnosis involves monitoring oxygen levels at a sleep clinic or at home.

Treatments for milder cases follow directly from the cause or causes for that person, e.g. losing weight or surgery on an injured nose. More severe cases need a mask that pumps air quite gently through the nostrils. This is uncomfortable and indeed intolerable for some people, but can dramatically improve quality of life for the snorer and other people affected.

Chapter 4

Memory problems and dementia

In this chapter, we consider how our mental abilities might change as we age and, in particular, the differences between forgetfulness, Mild Cognitive Impairment and dementia. We also consider the two most common types of dementia and support for people with dementia and their carers.

Mental abilities and age

How do people who are old differ in their mental abilities and characteristics from the young and middle-aged? Do they tend to be more forgetful? Slower to learn new skills? Confused? Calmer? Grumpier? Wiser?

In this section, we first note some of the numerous research findings on such questions and then focus on strategies for coping with those abilities that are declining, and retaining or improving the others. If you compare the findings with your observations of yourself and others, please bear in mind the following assessment from Patrick Rabbitt's 2015 book *The Aging Mind, an Owner's Manual* (Professor Rabbitt's spelling of ageing and ours are both correct). He wrote,

> The more closely we study age changes the better we recognise how slight they are, how very gradually they progress and how they can be slowed and ameliorated and what are the best steps we can take to cope with them.

Please therefore bear in mind that the slight differences in typical performance between groups of people of different ages conceal large individual differences and overlaps between the age groups. Age, in Rabbitt's expert view, is not a good indicator of ability.

Finding 1 – intelligence test results peak in the late teens or early
20s, remain constant for five to 10 years then decline slowly,
with a slow acceleration in people's 40s and 50s, accelerating
more sharply in their late 70s and 80s.

This statement is broadly true but complicated by varying patterns and different aspects of intelligence – for example, in some
people speed of making decisions has a pattern very like that of
general IQ scores, while other people's scores on this aspect of intelligence remain very similar throughout long lives. Much depends
on how intelligence is defined.

Finding 2 – older people are more likely to forget things like
where their keys, glasses etc. are and why they've gone into
another room.

This kind of forgetting is true of many people in other age groups
too, indeed of people in general.

Finding 3 – older people tend to forget words, especially people's names. The particular word or name won't appear, then
it suddenly does.

As with Finding 2, this is largely part of how memory works
and therefore true of people in general too. The differences between
forgetting in normal ageing, Mild Cognitive Impairment (MCI) and
dementia are discussed in the next section.

Finding 4 – older people can remember as long a list of ran-
dom numbers as younger people can. However, they tend to
remember them less well backwards and to be less able to
remember two sets of numbers when each is presented simultaneously to a different ear, when there is an interruption
between memorising and being asked to remember the lists,
or when trying to follow two or more conversations at once
(sometimes called the 'cocktail party phenomenon').

Rabbitt comments that old age 'sharply degrades' this aspect of
memory, so it is a rare exception to his general evaluation of the
differences as 'slight' and may well be familiar.
Findings 5–10 next are all slight differences.

Finding 5 – older people become less efficient at learning new things but can still learn.

Finding 6 – older people are more inventive/resourceful about strategies to help them cope with everyday memory problems.

Finding 7 – older people can remain competent in skills learnt earlier in life if they have continued to use them.

Finding 8 – older people are less able to distinguish between unfamiliar faces and between different facial expressions.

Finding 9 – older people report feeling happier.

Finding 10 – older people struggle more to stay alert when trying to do difficult tasks for long periods.

Forgetfulness and age

Forgetting in normal ageing

One of the things we just have to accept as we get older is that we may not be as mentally quick and agile as we once were. It is very understandable to jump to conclusions and worry that this must mean we are getting cognitive impairment or dementia and it could therefore be downhill all the way. This is not necessarily the case, as it is probably just normal ageing.

We generally wouldn't expect to be as physically quick and agile as we age, so most people cut themselves a bit of slack there and simply accept it as normal ageing. Somehow the changes in mental capacities can seem a bit more worrying, possibly because of the fear of dementia and not being able to live an independent life anymore.

Although the mental changes with normal ageing are a nuisance and they might irritate you or others, they are not bad enough to have a serious effect on your day-to-day life. You can still live an independent life, and you don't need to rely on others to stop the gap. Normal ageing changes include the following:

- forgetting things occasionally
- slower reactions, thinking things through and decision making – for example, not being able to multi-task as well as when we were younger, being a bit slower to process things or react or making ill-thought-through decisions sometimes
- communication problems – for example, taking a while to think of the right word, getting distracted in conversations and losing the thread sometimes

- changed energy levels and mood – for example, not having the energy or desire for some interpersonal meetings, not liking your routines interfered with, having the odd off-day when you just can't be bothered with certain things

All of these things can show up more when we are tired, ill or overloaded. This is another reason to prioritise getting fit and healthy and sleeping well – and to very carefully consider not taking on more than you can comfortably cope with. Just because we managed many roles and activities when younger doesn't mean we have to continue to do this as we get older. The assertive skill of 'saying no', discussed in Chapter 11, can be invaluable here.

Forgetting in Mild Cognitive Impairment (MCI)

This is diagnosed by a doctor if they consider someone to have more difficulties with their memory, thinking and mental processing than would be expected for someone the same age. So it is *more than* normal age-related changes, but it is not as severe as dementia and is not a form of dementia, although, like dementia, it becomes more common with age. Most people with MCI are over 70. There are various tests that doctors can do to help them make this diagnosis. It may be caused by some underlying conditions that can be treated – such as depression, a physical illness like thyroid disease or infections or problems with hearing and sight. All the lifestyle changes that reduce the risk of getting dementia (discussed later in this chapter) will also contribute to reducing the risk of getting MCI. Someone with MCI is at higher risk (than someone without MCI) of getting dementia later, but it is by no means inevitable.

There is no specific drug treatment for MCI, but living a healthier lifestyle helps cognitive functioning. There may be local support groups that your doctor can refer you to in order to help you manage day-to-day life issues and give support and encouragement for lifestyle changes. On a practical, daily level, there are many things that you can do to allow for any cognitive limitations and help you stay living as independently as possible. These will be things that keep you on top of daily routines and tasks and reduce some of the stress and anxiety the condition may cause.

A general strategy for coping with forgetting is to appreciate that it is an essential part of brains working well. Without it, we would be quickly overloaded by the huge amount of new information that we process every day. Instead, our brains select and interpret.

Moreover, not appreciating this and having recurring stressful thoughts about getting more forgetful can itself interfere with memory. Sometimes we make jokes about this, saying, for example, 'I'm pretty sure that's not an early sign of dementia'.

Two other general methods for improving our memories and other cognitive skills are to sleep well and to check the side effects of any medications. Then there are more specific ways of coping, e.g. repeating a new name shortly after being introduced to the person whose name it is; sticky notes and diaries; having pairs of glasses in more than one room; mnemonics; visualisation techniques, although some of us lack this ability or have it only weakly; and a healthy diet.

Psychological attempts at brain training in a general sense have been ineffective so far, though some of its techniques have been and are widely used. The idea of a 'brain gym' implies that it is just like physical training and so, it is claimed, develops cognitive abilities and also resists their decline as we get older. A sceptical position is generally held by researchers so far: that 'brain training' develops only the ability to do the particular exercises or games practised, that at best they can be fun to do and that they are unlikely to be harmful.

However, one strategy for improving mental skills is dramatically stronger than any other, much more effective than 'slight' in its effects on both physical and mental health, and inexpensive. This strategy is aerobic exercise.

Aerobic exercise

Aerobic exercise is regular physical exertion which results in heavy breathing and raised heart rate for a sustained period. You get sweaty and breathless, but you can still talk in phrases or sentences. It can be achieved in a variety of ways, the usual recommendations being walking, jogging, running, cycling, dancing, swimming, etc. Aerobic exercise benefits our physical fitness generally, e.g. heart and lungs, but also, and substantially, our brain health and therefore memory and other mental abilities.

One question about aerobic exercise is the optimum level of exertion for increasing or maintaining good health. Our position is, as stated in the five principles at the beginning of Chapter 1, in general terms, to compete with yourself at a comfortable and enjoyable level rather than strive to meet a level which is a guess and at best an average, for example 10,000 steps and eight glasses of fluid a day. However, we realise that for some of us, competing with others or with a standard set by others is very enjoyable and motivating, and we suggest that if this is true of you that you also emphasise self-care in an assertive way (Chapter 11). In particular, we want you to judge well when you need to rest.

We also recommend checking with your GP or other appropriately qualified health professional that what you propose to do is likely to be safe and effective for you.

Dementia

The thought of getting dementia is frightening. It is not just the fear of getting it yourself, but also the concern about a partner or loved one becoming demented and you taking on the role of carer. These fears are entirely understandable as it is never what anyone wants in old age – one's world can be turned upside down by a diagnosis of dementia.

This is a good reason to become more familiar with dementia and what can be done to prevent it or manage it.

Risk factors

- The biggest risk factor is age – it is more common over the age of 65 and the risk of being diagnosed with it increases with each decade. Although it is estimated that about one in six people over 80 get it, this still means that five out of six people don't, which is the vast majority.
- Overall, more women than men get dementia, and certain ethnic groups are more at risk – African, Afro-Caribbean and South Asian people have higher rates than white Europeans.
- Inheriting it is very unlikely – and in these rare cases, it is usually in people under 65. So just because your parent had it in old age doesn't mean you will get it too.
- All the things that affect heart and cardiovascular system health will also affect your brain health. About one in three cases of dementia are now thought to be preventable, and risk factors that can be changed include poor physical health, smoking, obesity, lack of exercise, high alcohol intake, high blood pressure and diabetes.

Types of dementia

Dementia is a term used to describe a set of symptoms that occur when brain function is affected by an underlying progressive disease.

The symptoms can vary in each type of dementia and in each individual person, but they generally are to do with:

- memory problems
- thinking and communicating problems
- confusion and disorientation
- changes in personality and mood swings

There are many different types of dementia, but the most common types are Alzheimer's disease and vascular dementia. Dementia with Lewy bodies and frontotemporal dementia are two examples of the rarer types of dementia. Some people have a mix of types of dementia – most commonly a mix of Alzheimer's disease and vascular dementia.

Alzheimer's disease

This is the most common type in the UK and is associated with a build-up of protein-based 'plaques' and 'tangles' in the brain. These interfere with the proper functioning of nerve cells in the brain and eventually cause death of some of the cells. In addition, there is disrupted chemical messaging in the brain.

Alzheimer's disease usually comes on slowly, often with mild memory loss. This progresses, and other symptoms such as difficulty with language, confusion and changes in personality or mood swings can occur. The slow pace allows for years of interesting and productive life, especially with carers who understand the need of the person with dementia for sameness in their surroundings and routine. This aspect of dementia is vividly described by Wendy Mitchell in her book *Somebody I Used to Know*, and Nicci Gerrard in *What Dementia Teaches Us about Love*. Also recommended are not arguing with or correcting the accuracy of the person with dementia's statements and instead focusing on their emotions and topics that interest them, e.g. on reminiscences stimulated by a photo or piece of music and the other activities recommended in the section on non-drug treatments later in this chapter.

Vascular dementia

This dementia is due to interrupted blood supply to the brain, which can cause brain cells to die. Vascular changes can be caused by a stroke (called post-stroke dementia) or after a series of mini-strokes (called multi-infarct dementia). Another variant is subcortical vascular dementia, which is due to poor blood supply to deep parts of the brain.

Vascular dementia can come on either suddenly or in stages, and the symptoms depend on which part of the brain has been damaged. However, common early symptoms are problems with thinking and planning and difficulty concentrating. There may also be changes in mood. Unlike Alzheimer's disease, memory loss is not such a common early feature.

Getting a diagnosis of dementia

If you are worried about early signs of dementia in yourself or a partner, then see your GP. GPs are the first point of call for getting a diagnosis of dementia and excluding other potential causes of dementia-like symptoms. Sometimes conditions such as infections, thyroid disease or depression can affect memory, thinking skills and behaviour and can look like dementia.

Your GP may refer you on to a memory clinic or another hospital specialist for further investigations. Getting a correct diagnosis is important as it then allows you to access the dementia support services in your area and get treatment, if applicable, as early as possible.

Treatments

Sadly, there is no known cure, as yet, for dementia. Treatments that are available are to alleviate symptoms and to slow down the progress of symptoms.

There are four main approaches:

- drug treatments for the chemical changes in Alzheimer's disease (and sometimes other rarer dementias)
- drug treatments for underlying conditions that cause vascular dementia (such as hypertension, high cholesterol, diabetes, etc.); the specific dementia drugs for Alzheimer's disease don't work for vascular dementia
- lifestyle changes to try to limit the progression of vascular dementia (this would be all the things that help the underlying conditions, for example not smoking, eating a healthy diet and getting enough exercise)
- non-drug treatments of dementia

There are a number of approaches that help to stimulate your brain and help improve quality of life for people with dementia.

Examples are:

- Music, dancing and creative arts – sessions are led by a professional either one to one or in groups. Engaging in these activities can help stimulate the brain and improve mood and expressiveness. It has been shown that memory for music and songs can remain relatively unaffected by dementia.
- Cognitive stimulation therapy – this can be a set of different activities (word puzzles, music, talking about memories or current affairs, etc.) aimed at stimulating brain function and improving some dementia symptoms.
- Cognitive rehabilitation – where people with dementia can work with a professional in order to achieve a particular goal that would be useful. This could be a practical skill or learning something new.
- Looking back at your life history and reminiscence activities – working one to one with someone else on memories from the past is a useful way of improving memory, mood and general wellbeing.

Prevention – keeping your brain healthy

All the things that we can do to stay generally fit and healthy will have a positive impact on our brain health and help prevent or delay dementia.

It is not too late to adopt a healthier lifestyle as we age. This includes the following general points:

- eating a healthy diet (see the section on diet in Chapter 2)
- maintaining a healthy weight
- not smoking
- moderating alcohol intake
- staying physically active
- keeping up with social activities and friendships – in groups as well as one to one (this requires concerted, active management as we age, as we may not have as many social interactions available 'on tap' as we might have had when we were younger, perhaps from a job or immediate family).
- doing things that stimulate your brain and use different parts of your brain – a variety of hobbies and activities that you enjoy and that keep you engaged and active (learning a language, for example, can be a great all-round brain stimulator)

- making sure any underlying health issues you may have are being actively managed by you and your doctor, especially conditions like diabetes, high blood pressure and high blood cholesterol

Support for people with dementia and their carers

Most people will have little knowledge of what services are available for people who are diagnosed with dementia or their carers, unless they have been directly affected by it already, perhaps when an elderly parent had dementia.

Seek advice from your GP on what services there are in your area. These can include:

- **Health services** – these can include a range of nurses and allied health professionals who may help with specific needs related to your physical and mental health.
- **Social services** – including a range of services from help around the house and making living arrangements safer and more dementia friendly to providing places in day centres and support groups. You would need to contact your local authority social services to arrange an assessment of your needs. They can then set up a support plan to address your needs.
- **Charities and not-for-profit sector** – national organisations such as Age UK, Dementia UK, Alzheimer's Society, Carers UK and Carers Trust can be very helpful sources of information about dementia and also can signpost you to their local and national services. These range from dementia advisors, nurses and support groups to day centres and advocacy services.
- **Specific support for carers** – it is very important to find out what advice and support there is in your local area to help you if you are in a carer's role. It is easy to gradually take on a carer role and not realise the rising toll this may have on your mental and physical health. When the focus is mainly on the person with dementia, it is easy to lose focus on your own needs. Not only can your GP be of help and ensure you are on the practice carer's register, but they can also advise you of other services that may assist. Social services, for example, can arrange a carer's assessment to help map out what care and assistance you may need in your caring role. Many of the charities mentioned previously have specific support and advice for people in a caring role; for example, Dementia UK Admiral nurses can support families who are looking after a loved one with dementia.

Chapter 5

Looking after your health

Patients as active participants in decisions about their healthcare

Our aim in this chapter is to help patients who wish to be more active in consultations about their health with health professionals. This approach is consistent with the 2018 guidance from the Academy of Medical Royal Colleges on the kinds of information that should be discussed in consultations. To summarise these, the Academy uses the acronym BRAN, which stands for Benefits, Risks, Alternative treatments and the likely consequences if you choose to do Nothing – the wait and see option.

Taking an active approach requires being assertive with health professionals, as in these examples from two patients. The first is about an underlying attitude, which would probably make assertive behaviour more likely; the second is an example of expressing that attitude.

First patient: 'I believe in standing up for myself and asking for details and a second opinion if it feels like a good idea. I understand that the staff are very busy, but it's my health that's at stake here'.

The second patient put a big card at the head of her hospital bed that read:

Who are you?
What is your job?
What treatments are you considering for me?
Are there other possibilities?

Each of these examples will appeal more to some people than others, but they illustrate the spirit of patients being active participants in decisions about their health and can clarify how assertive we ourselves might want to be. Here, two central considerations are 1) the final assertive right of those listed in Chapter 11: that we have the right *not* to be assertive, and 2) that the aim is for patients and health professionals to listen respectfully to each other and indeed to collaborate. The information in the rest of this chapter is intended to contribute towards such discussions between patients and health professionals.

To the same end, the National Institute for Health and Care Excellence (nice.org.uk) provides detailed guidelines for treating some illnesses, and health professionals are expected usually to implement these with the informed agreement of the patient or their representative. Health professionals may also use their clinical judgement, but if they don't follow the NICE guidance may have to justify their decision to colleagues or professional organisations. The NICE guidance is available on the internet in two forms: for the general public and for health professionals. We suggest consulting both forms.

Next we discuss four further aspects of medical treatment, knowledge of which can contribute to being an active participant on behalf of ourselves or others: doctor-patient communication, prescription drugs, health screening and miracle cures.

Consulting a doctor

Years ago, there were older people who were reluctant to 'bother the doctor' and would struggle on, trying to sort out their symptoms themselves. It may be difficult to believe this now that many GP surgeries are bursting at the seams with patient requests to be seen – and some people have to wait weeks before they can get a routine appointment.

Most older people have now lived most of their lives with a UK NHS system in place, so the old potential reticence about seeking help from a doctor (who had to be paid) has diminished, and there are higher expectations of what our healthcare system can offer us.

However, going to see a doctor is not necessarily a straightforward thing – and the following points may be helpful for older people who need medical help:

1   Some people are still rather reticent about consulting a doctor for various reasons – not wanting to bother them may be still partly an issue, but also there may be an element of not wanting to face up to whatever symptom is bothering them and what it might really mean to their health and life. The truth is that GPs

are there to be of help: that's their job, and they want patients to come to them with their health worries. Most of them would rather be consulted earlier when treatment might be easier or more effective, rather than wait for things to get much more serious. GPs also understand that a part of their job is helping people who are the 'worried well', who don't actually have any serious health issues but need their reassurance nonetheless.

2   After the birth of the internet and the copious information on health issues that anyone could easily get hold of, some people would arrive at their doctor's surgery with an armful of paper, convinced that they were up to date with the latest information on what they believed was wrong with them. While it must be a little frustrating for doctors to be presumed less knowledge-able on medical matters than their patients, there is a balance to be had here. It is a good idea to do a bit of homework on your health concern before seeing your doctor – mainly so you can understand the area better and think of what questions you may wish to ask your doctor. It may help to write down all the questions you have so that you don't forget to ask when you are under the spotlight. Doing a bit of homework may also give you a better idea of the range of healthcare practitioners who deal with different aspects of care of your condition. Many people, understandably, have no idea what healthcare services are available to them until they need them.

3   If you are particularly worried about your situation and think you won't be able to take on board what your doctor might say, or don't feel you'll remember to ask enough questions, then take a friend or relative with you into the consultation room as an extra pair of ears and eyes. They may help to jot things down to help you remember and act as some moral support at an anxious time.

4   If you are referred to a specialist at a hospital, then, again, it may help to do a bit of homework on understanding that part of the NHS. All NHS Trusts have websites that explain how services are delivered, who is in that department and who else works alongside them. Many services are now grouped into condition-specific clinical networks where all the relevant healthcare providers work together to offer a more seamless service for patients – for example, cancer networks and cardiac networks.

5   In some situations, you may want to get a second opinion. It doesn't necessarily mean you would need to pay for a private consultation – you could ask to see someone else in your area of the NHS. Before doing this, make sure you've asked all the questions you are worried about and that you're as satisfied with the first doctor's answers as seems realistic. Some people worry about appearing pushy or a nuisance and taking up time, but it is fine to ensure you're satisfied with your diagnosis and care. Don't assume that going privately will mean better care than in NHS settings – any doctor should be working to the latest clinical guidelines.

Prescription drugs

Prescription drugs can save lives but, like screening, diagnostic procedures and other treatments and operations, they come with risks as well as benefits.

Part of your doctor's job is to assess whether the benefits of taking a prescription drug are likely to outweigh the risks for you. There are some categories of drugs which can have quite severe side effects, dependence issues or withdrawal problems. Examples are opioids (used as pain killers), benzodiazepines and some antidepressants. The days of anxious housewives being dependent on benzodiazepines (like Valium) due to over-zealous prescribing are fortunately mainly a thing of the past. However, there are still many patients who put off taking or continuing with antidepressants, for example, because of intolerable side effects.

Patients who are concerned about the side effects and withdrawal problems of taking a drug they are prescribed can take some or all of the following steps:

1   Look up the prescribed drug on MedlinePlus and the NHS website. The most relevant information to look for is generally 1) how long on average it takes to have the various benefits, 2) the most likely side effects and the most serious, 3) whether starting with a lower dose than the standard one is feasible – older people tend to be less able to metabolise drugs, and the standard dosage is usually based on samples of young, healthy males, and 4) any problems with dependence and the resulting difficulties with stopping taking the drug.

2   Ask your GP about any of the answers you found that you wonder about, plus the risks of not taking it, and possible interactions with other drugs you are taking, including herbal medicines. Older people tend to take more than one drug at a time, and indeed five drugs is quite common. This is partly because some drugs, e.g. statins, are prescribed to millions of people to try to prevent particular illnesses, and some are treatments for side effects of others.

A lot of these questions are answered by the leaflets enclosed with prescription drugs. This information is clear but understandably very concise, and by the time you get the leaflet you may already have the drug and may decide not to take it. It will then be wasted – the NHS spends many millions of pounds a year on subscriptions for people who do not take their prescriptions, a decision which may be healthier for these patients but is very wasteful for the NHS.

Safe withdrawal from some prescription drugs

Large numbers of patients are dependent on the antidepressants, pain killers and benzodiazepines mentioned earlier. Professor Heather C. Ashton's Manual, which is available free on her website, benzo.org.uk, is a very clear, practical and authoritative guide to withdrawing safely from benzodiazepines, e.g. clonazepam and Valium. It also illustrates the principles of safe withdrawal from addictive drugs generally. The central element is making very small reductions at the right pace for the individual patient while treating withdrawal symptoms like nausea, insomnia and rebound anxiety if necessary.

Avoiding prescription drugs

Many health conditions are caused by or made worse by our lifestyle choices. It makes sense to target the *cause* of our condition if at all possible, rather than just treat the symptoms with drugs. Having a prescription written for symptoms is the quickest route, but proper advice and support on lifestyle changes can take much more time and patience, for both the health professional and the patient. Many of the major disease issues for older people have a recognised lifestyle element to them, and this is included in clinical guidelines for the management of the condition. In many cases, lifestyle changes are advised to be tried first rather than going straight to medication. Examples are the prevention of cardiovascular disease and prevention and treatment of type 2 diabetes.

As an active participant in our health, it is important to recognise the degree of influence we have over our health and healthcare choices. Actively focusing on our lifestyle and getting the support needed to make healthy changes can make all the difference, not just to how we feel each day but to how many drugs we have to take. It is not a foregone conclusion that older people need to be on a medley of prescription drugs.

Health screening

The intuitive appeal of screening

It is understandable why people want to be screened. Mainly it is because they want to be reassured that they don't have a potentially serious health problem. There's enough in life to worry about, and so getting tested or screened can help many people allay their fears and worries about their health. Intuitively, it makes sense that if diseases can be picked up early enough, then they can be more easily treated. This becomes even more pressing if the person has experience of someone close to them, maybe a relative or friend, who has had the disease or died of it. All of this can blinker people to the whole picture of screening, including its potential downside.

However, it is very important to recognise that screening is a balancing act: overall, is it likely to produce more benefit than harm? This is why screening needs to be taken very seriously and why, for example, the UK NHS set up a robust system for evaluating potential screening tests and programmes. The UK National Screening Committee (NSC) is the NHS body that oversees policy on screening. It ensures that the science and evidence have been thoroughly assessed before a screening test or programme is recommended for use on NHS patients.

It publishes on its website a list of conditions for which potential screening tests or programmes have been assessed. These are regularly updated as more evidence or decisions become available. Current (2020) recommended screening programmes for adults are:

- abdominal aortic aneurysm (AAA) (men over 65)
- bowel cancer (men and women 50–74)
- breast cancer (women over 50)
- cervical cancer (women 25–64)
- diabetic retinopathy (for people with diabetes)

See legacyscreening.phe.org.uk for the latest information on screening programmes and www.gov.uk/phe/screening-leaflets.

Accepted principles for healthcare screening

Screening is a balancing act between the potential benefits it can give and the potential harms. This is the case for any healthcare intervention, but the difference with screening is that it is healthy, asymptomatic people who are usually offered it. This makes it even more important that the benefits outweigh the harms. There are a number of accepted principles of screening that health professionals should subscribe to:

- Only offer screening if there is proven evidence that, overall, the benefits of screening outweigh the potential harms. This means that screening should *not* be offered if there is evidence suggesting that screening is *not beneficial* or there is *absence of known evidence* (i.e. either the research is not sufficient yet or it hasn't been properly assessed against all the good practice screening criteria).
- Screening should only be offered if it can fulfil the relevant list of criteria for a worthwhile screening programme. These are well-established criteria, accepted by the World Health Organisation. The NHS National Screening Committee uses an expanded version of them to appraise all potential screening programmes.

The potential pitfalls of screening

Not knowing enough about the potential downside of screening

There are two great problems concerning the *downside* of screening and testing. The first is that not many people know about the downside or understand it. The second is that many proponents (and sellers) of screening tend to play it down or don't mention it much at all – instead they are more interested in the potential benefits. There is probably a third problem as well – if a patient is particularly anxious to be reassured about their health, they might choose to turn a blind eye to potential harms of screening.

The following are examples of issues that need to be considered before undergoing screening.

How important is the condition being screened for?

There is little point screening for conditions:

- that aren't really all that significant to one's health
- that could be more easily prevented in the first place
- where not much is known about the natural history of that disease (e.g. how rapidly it progresses in most people and how often it is very serious or fatal)
- where there is no known proven treatment or no agreed treatment

Offering screening for these sorts of conditions or diseases is likely to be of no real benefit to the patient. It may be wasting their time and raising false hopes and expectations. There's little point offering screening when it is not clear whether it will really make a difference to their health and when it is not clear how any disease picked up will be treated. If early diagnosis does not result in better health outcomes, then really all one is doing is giving someone a diagnosis to worry about for longer (and possibly subjecting them to a host of investigations and invasive treatments along the way).

Is the screening test good enough?

- Screening should be avoided if the screening test has not been properly tested for safety and the screening test is not sufficiently precise or accurate. Not all screening tests are harmless – it is possible to have a test that, in itself, is too risky to perform on otherwise well people.
- The screening test is not very good at detecting the condition (so produces too many false negative results, i.e. missed cases). This can lead to false reassurance. As a result of this, people might stop making an effort to keep up their healthy habits and

behaviours. They may think they are no longer at risk. Examples are drinking habits, smoking, exercise and diet. This could therefore put them at even greater risk of the disease being screened for.

- The screening test is not very good at sorting out who *hasn't* got the disease (so produces too many false positive results). This can lead to people having to be referred on for further investigations and diagnostic tests when they are actually disease-free. Not only does this cause anxiety, but also the investigations and diagnostic measures can be quite invasive and even have their own risks and side effects. For example, prostate biopsies might be required for patients who have a raised PSA test, and there is a risk involved in this. One of the reasons why it took a long time for the NHS to decide to run the bowel cancer screening programme was because of the risk that is involved in carrying out colonoscopies on patients who are FOB (faecal occult blood) test–positive.

Screening is only worthwhile if it gives a measurable benefit to the patients screened. The most obvious benefit is if screening stops people dying from the disease. There is little point picking up diseases early if there is no effective early treatment available that can make a real difference to that person's health. If the outcomes for screen-detected patients are no better than those of patients who present later on with symptoms, then screening is not worthwhile.

Sometimes the research shows differing benefits for different age groups or sexes – e.g. abdominal aortic aneurysm screening is only considered worthwhile for men aged 65 and older – screening women and people younger than 65 does not give an overall benefit to patients and may even on balance do them more harm than good.

When patients who are otherwise healthy go for screening tests, they may end up with a test result or diagnosis that not only causes them anxiety but can also mean that other things are affected that they hadn't even considered. For example, their insurance status, employment opportunities and medical fitness to carry out certain activities (e.g. driving or operating certain machinery) might be affected if they or their doctor are asked to declare their health status. This may be considered a worthwhile downside if the overall results of screening benefit the patient's health and life, but it would be a significant drawback that needs considering if there are no other benefits obtained from screening.

There is little point picking up potential problems if there are no agreed ways of investigating them further. There needs to be agreement right along the screening 'pathway' about who is going to do what with screen-positive patients. Otherwise, patients' anxieties will be raised that they have a positive result, but then they will not be investigated and diagnosed in a streamlined and efficient way.

Miracle cures – what works?

The modern digital world is full of information only a few clicks away. Being able to instantly 'Google' the answer to almost any question is taken for granted these days. It is easy to see the advantages of this international storehouse of information, but there are clear downsides when you are looking for answers to health questions.

It is worth considering the following broad points when trying to find out if something is all it's cracked up to be.

Advertising and marketing

Don't confuse good advertising and promotion with actual product efficacy. There is an art and science to marketing, and although it is illegal to sell things on false claims, there are some grey areas where it comes to health products. Some years ago, there was a crackdown in the UK on how certain 'alternative' products were marketed, and they were no longer able to make health claims on the packaging and information leaflets. Many had to label themselves as 'traditional treatments' and were not allowed to make bolder claims of efficacy on health-related conditions. Despite this, if there is a good advertising campaign or convincing, appealing packaging, it is easy to believe that the product must be good.

Beware the source

In pre-internet times, it was perhaps easier to see who or what the source of information was and make your own assessment. Having someone in a pub spouting his latest theory on x, y or z was at least overt, and many people would take it with a large pinch of salt. But when everything is in printed format and appears on an impressive-looking website, it can be more difficult to see through it so readily. Anyone can set up a website on their PC at the kitchen table, and say they are an international company and experts in whatever they choose. They may have almost no credibility under scrutiny, but on your computer screen they look as authentic as the next one. It is wise to check out other sources of information, and even though there has been a lot of 'expert bashing' in recent years, there is some comfort in listening to more traditional sources of information, where there is professional regulation and peer scrutiny. Sometimes the old saying is helpful – 'if it sounds too good to be true, then it probably is'.

Organised systems for reviewing health information in the UK

In the UK, there are well-established, non-commercial organisations and bodies whose purpose is to systematically review published literature on given health subjects. These use tightly run methods that seek out and sift through a myriad of published information, make sense of it and report the findings so that they are usable for policy makers and clinicians. These often involve 'meta-analysis', which is a way of combining the results of individual studies to produce one statistic. There are strict criteria for what is considered acceptable data and what is not. The work is done by trained experts in data review and analysis, overseen by independent panels of experienced professionals in the relevant fields as well as lay members.

Examples are the National Institute for Health and Care Excellence, NICE (which is a public body funded by the Department of Health and Social Care), and the Cochrane Library and its Reviews (which are independently funded and non-commercial). The reviews often include a health economics view of the subject, as many new treatments are expensive and the question needs to be addressed – is this treatment worth it in terms of its cost, relative to its reported outcomes for patients? Unless a health system has an unlimited budget, decisions have to be made on which treatments or prevention programmes are the most worthwhile, relative to everything else that requires funding.

Although these reviews are mainly aimed at professionals, they are published and accessible to all on the web and in printed format. Some of the detail will, of course, be beyond the general understanding of a lay person, but they are usually written in plain English, and the summaries and recommendations are clear enough for most people to comprehend.

Other useful sources of information are the reports of expert committees on specific health subjects that are produced by the various Royal Colleges and Faculties for different healthcare professionals (e.g. the Royal College of Physicians, the Royal College of Psychiatrists, the Royal College of Nursing). Again, many of these are accessible on the web to everyone, and summaries and conclusions will be generally understandable by a lay person.

Lack of evidence or evidence of lack?

There is a big difference between these two, and yet they often end up conflated. Some reviews of the literature are able to show that there is little or no benefit for certain health treatments or preventive measures. This is based on published data and is a useful finding that can guide your healthcare decisions. This is evidence of lack (of effectiveness).

However, there is a wide range of things for which there is simply lack of sufficient evidence with which to make a decision on effectiveness and outcomes. The reason for this can be because good-enough research has simply not been done or published. There have been many discussions in academic circles about the implicit bias to publish research that has positive results, and so research that shows that something doesn't work is considered less interesting or newsworthy.

Another reason for lack of evidence is that the thing being looked at is inherently difficult to study – perhaps because it is difficult to strictly define or standardise treatments or find suitable controls or dummy treatments to compare it with. This can also cause difficulty obtaining research grants. A bigger problem is where the treatment or intervention is working in a different type of paradigm, i.e. one that is outside the usual biomedical model that most doctors use. Examples here are research on things that are primarily working on an energetic level rather than a material level, such as acupuncture and homeopathy. Interestingly, physicists are scientists who continually have to review their notions of what is possible and acceptable – as they expand their knowledge and start to look sub-atomically, they find that solid matter is no longer relevant and energy, waves or fields become more appropriate. Traditional western medicine hasn't quite kept pace with this 'physics open-mindedness' despite the increasing use of many diagnostic and treatment techniques that are almost entirely modern physics–based, like MRI (magnetic resonance imaging) scanning.

This lack-of-evidence issue can therefore leave a type of 'knowledge vacuum', and it is easy for people to rush to fill it with their own theories and claims. It is also easy for others to say that something is rubbish or quackery, based on prejudice and lack of data. This leaves the lay person in a difficult position of having to make their own mind up. Some people are more open to understanding different, alternative paradigms and are happy to look at older, traditional healthcare approaches such as acupuncture, Ayurveda or homeopathy.

Ultimately, it is prudent to take a balanced view and trust your own judgement based on your own experiences, and only try things that are unlikely to cause you harm.

Social and psychological aspects of getting old

Chapter 6

Attitudes towards getting old

Much has been written on this topic, but it is not examined and discussed as overtly as it should be in everyday life. It largely remains implicit and often hides in the shadows of assumption and prejudice. The Equality Act of 2010 in England and Wales has nine strands of equality, and one of them is age. Although it is illegal to discriminate against people purely based on their age, it is difficult to enforce this on a day-to-day basis, especially in multi-factored situations where you can't quite put your finger on what is going on. Overt age discrimination in more formal settings (like job interviews) may be easier to detect and deal with, but the subtler, everyday experiences of age discrimination and prejudice often fly below the radar. It is much the same for the other aspects of equality where people are more likely to be discriminated against, like gender and ethnicity, for example. Of course, for an individual, they are always the sum of many parts – and it can be difficult to untangle the effects. The day-to-day experiences of, say, an older, Asian woman of lower socio-economic class in the UK will no doubt be very different from those of a middle-aged, white, middle-class man.

One way of looking at this in a personal context is to consider firstly what seems to be the attitude of others towards getting old and, secondly, what your own attitude to ageing is.

Others' attitudes towards getting old

Others' attitudes are both from your more 'immediate others' (the people you directly live and work with) and the culture and society you live in. It is difficult to live in a culture that exhibits negative attitudes towards ageing and not absorb some or all of it. The reason that age is part of the Equality Act is because it is an undeniable, active area of prejudice and discrimination in our culture. We are culturally looking at people though 'age-tinted' lenses that distort and diminish the reality. This is an area that is included in studies in sociology, psychology, politics, economics, marketing, philosophy and more – asking why, as a society, do we diminish and devalue people simply based on their age? What's wrong with getting old?

Like other aspects of life, we often aren't aware of the degree of the issue until it actually affects *us* or someone very close to us. For example, most people don't notice the difficulty of accessing a particular building for someone with limited mobility or in a wheelchair. So much of life can be taken for granted – until, sometimes suddenly, it can't. Ageing happens gradually, but many people may remember the first time they noticed an effect of being discriminated against or just treated differently due to their age.

Sometimes it is simply feeling 'invisible'. Some older women, in particular, may remember the first time this happened – either standing at a busy bar trying to get served or walking down a street and feeling what it is like to be unnoticed. This can be particularly strange if, when younger, they had a sense of being 'attractive' and responded to. On the other hand, some women may rather enjoy their newfound invisibility and being left alone and no longer 'eyed up'.

If one looks hard enough, there are no doubt many examples of subtle discrimination against older people in, for example, goods, services and policies. Caroline Creado-Perez's excellent book *Invisible Women* recently won the prestigious Royal Society science book award. She describes how much of life is 'one size fits men' – and shows examples of everyday bias against women in many areas of design and policy. A similar book could be written focusing on age rather than gender, and it would be interesting to overtly uncover the implicit everyday bias against older people. Most if it is probably mainly because the needs of older people are simply not kept in mind. It is highly unlikely to be a positive effort to exclude, discriminate or show disregard to older people. Examples of 'everyday disregard' are making the assumption that everyone is able to conduct their affairs online with access to a computer or smartphone; not supplying frequent-enough buses for out-of-town locations; or designing packaging for products with use instructions in a tiny, pale and therefore illegible font.

Sometimes it is something as basic as language that belies prejudice. We, all of us, need to notice and modify our use of ageist language, e.g. 'you're moaning like an old woman', 'the place was full of little old ladies', 'they were just a bunch of old biddies', and so on. These examples also add the familiar gender element too.

It is interesting how languages differ in describing age. In Italian, for example, one doesn't ask 'how old are you?'; they literally say, 'how many years do you have?' The reply is, 'I have x years'. Saying 'I have 70 years' (*ho settante anni*) feels less defining than 'I *am* 70' – it is more of a useful acquisition than an identity. Defining ourselves simply as a number is reductive; human beings are so much more than that. Similarly, filling in forms can make one feel very simply 'categorised'. Instead of having an occupation and being asked what it is, older people are often forced into ticking the box that simply says 'retired'. A retired *what* is not required – just 'retired'.

These things may seem subtle and, arguably, trivial in isolation, but they all add up to an overall 'drip, drip, drip' felt sense that can be very uncomfortable. This is why it is important for us to look to more positive examples of ageing and the real-life advantages it can bring, being more aware of societies and cultures that have a more respectful and honoured attitude to 'having years'. It is also why it is advantageous for us all to find and keep in mind positive role models for ageing and to make our own inventory of all the benefits of ageing. How we manage our own personal attitudes to ageing can make all the difference.

Our own attitude towards getting old

Our own attitude will be a mix of our general, intrinsic beliefs, assumptions and experiences about getting old plus the conditioned beliefs and judgements that we absorb from the world around us. Our environment no doubt shapes our own beliefs, but we do have some choice in the personal arena. We don't have to accept the attitudes of others and make them our own. We don't have to behave as if they were true.

It may help to put your own beliefs and attitudes under the spotlight. What *do* you believe about getting old? The trouble with personal beliefs is that they *feel true*, like facts – but the reality is they may not be. This is both good news and bad news. The good news is that we can decide if our current beliefs and attitudes are empowering and helpful to our lives or not. If not, then consider what would be a more empowering and helpful belief to have instead. Who do we know who has a more helpful belief system than we do – and how does that work for them? We can work out what we have to think and feel, and so start to change our beliefs. It is hard work and requires a lot of support, encouragement and practice, but it is worth it.

The bad news is that many people can feel unsettled and rather rattled at the prospect of unpicking beliefs they've lived by for a very long time. This can be especially difficult if you are surrounded by significant people in your life who feel rather threatened by you changing. Getting around people who have more empowering attitudes and habits about ageing may not only inspire you, but is likely to support and encourage your change of attitude too.

The evidence suggests that getting good at anything requires the triad of 1) opportunity, 2) support and encouragement and 3) practice, practice, practice. (See *Bounce* by Matthew Syed for an excellent overview of this.) Sometimes we have to actively stop doing things that keep us stuck in outdated attitudes. We may need to be very discerning about what external influences we allow in – what we read, what we watch, what we listen to, who we mix with. Importantly, we have to catch ourselves in the moment when we are doing things that are coming from old belief and attitude systems.

Chapter 7

Being oneself

Who are you and what do you want? People might assume these questions become redundant as we age, expecting we should know who we are and what we want by now. We have had so much time and experience in order to get to know ourselves. However, the question remains just as important. Ageing provides us with a golden opportunity to review everything that went before and decide what works for us now and who we really are at this point in our life.

Building a picture of yourself

This is perhaps an even better time to decide who we are and live it in reality rather than just in our idealistic fantasy world. The 'when . . . then' strategy of a conditional life in the future time expires itself as we age. The relevant question becomes: 'if not now, then when?' There is no longer a lifetime's worth of 'when' opportunities left, and this can focus the mind and, hopefully, spur on some action.

A lot has been written about mid-life transitions – they are a more accepted part of life, although often the butt of jokes and cringe-worthy stereotypes. But what about older people's transitions and explorations into their own identity? One way of looking at this is by boiling it down to two aspects: *knowledge* and *action*.

Knowledge

It is useful to review what we already know about ourselves and also to fill in the gaps. The song 'If You Don't Know Me by Now' might come to mind – and other people who don't have much appetite for self-examination and reflection may scoff at the idea of, say, a 70-year-old seriously wondering who they are. Ignore them.

The following is a list of areas to get curious about, find out about or revisit. Pulling it all together enables you to build an 'inventory' of yourself.

Personality

This is covered in detail later in this chapter. Being familiar with your own personality preferences (in the technical sense of that term) and the preferences of others helps you understand a host of things about yourself – how you like to communicate, make decisions, energise yourself, arrange your daily life and so on. Sometimes you can see that you may be wired up very differently from many other people, and it helps to understand that these are just normal differences and are not wrong. If you have spent your life so far feeling like a square peg in a round hole, then now can be a time to start making more congruent choices and looking for 'you-shaped' holes. It is energising to be living life in a way that fits with your personality. There are always things in life that we don't necessarily like or are not our strong suit, and we have to 'flex' to deal with them. What we want to avoid, however, is feeling like we are so constantly flexed that we are almost permanently bent out of shape.

Values

This is covered in detail later in this chapter. Being clear about our personal values helps us to make better, more appropriate choices in later life – choices that both feel right and make complete sense to us. They also provide a way of checking in from time to time to see if important things are aligned and as we want them to be.

Strengths

This is covered in detail later in this chapter. Identifying, appreciating and utilising our strengths can be a great boost and support as we age. Sometimes we have taken these aspects of ourselves for granted – so now is a good time to more consciously focus on them.

Interests/skills/energisers

Take a blank sheet of paper and write down:

- all the things (big or small) that you get a sense of pleasure or satisfaction from
- all the things that you can get so enjoyably engaged in that you don't notice time passing
- all the things you loved doing as a child
- all the things you love doing with other people
- all the things you most enjoy doing alone
- what other people who know you well say are your best attributes and skills
- what sort of television programmes or films you are drawn to
- what books or magazines or online sites you would most like to read on a long journey
- what topics of conversation you find most energising
- what you can easily turn your hand to
- what you can easily turn your mind to

Home and environment choices

Be curious about what sorts of things you are drawn to. What sort of colours do you like, how do you like to decorate your living spaces and what is important to you in your environment? What type of home would you most like and where? What sort of neighbours and locality do you like?

Clothes choices

What sort of clothes do you feel most comfortable in and what makes you feel most like you? How we dress as we get older is just as important as before – if anything, we can have a wider choice as there is a freedom that comes with age that can liberate us from the expectations and 'rules' to do with dressing. The truth is, most people are usually so wrapped up in themselves that they don't really notice or care about what you wear. It is a good opportunity to have a real clear-out and re-assessment of what works for you now. If you really want to wear purple and a red hat that doesn't go, then do it. If you feel more at home in muted colours and little adornment, then do that. Not everyone wants to look like Iris Apfel or Quentin

Crisp as they age, and there is no rule to say the only way older people will be noticed is if they are wearing very unconventional, brightly coloured clothes and accessories.

Attitude to life

What bon mots most appeal to you? If you had to be summed up in three to five words, what would they be? What would someone who knows you well say is your attitude to life? If a Martian came down, curious about people who live on Earth, and secretly watched you closely for a week, how would they report back to their fellow Martians?

Things that stress you/things you loathe

Think about two occasions when you felt really stressed. What was going on, and how did it affect you? What might it be telling you about those things in life that you simply don't like and want to avoid? Are there certain situations or experiences that you know you loathe? Why do you think that is? Clearly, there are some things in life that are worth rising to the challenge about and trying to overcome or deal with. However, as we age, it is also good to know when enough is enough and be clear about what you no longer want to tolerate in your life, given the choice. The good thing is that we usually do have more choice than we realise.

Relational choices

This is about what sort of relationships you like – how many people, how close they are and what sort of people you like to have in your life. It is amusing when so-called celebrities say they are having a small celebration (e.g. a wedding) and are inviting only 200 of their closest friends. How anyone can have 200 'close' friends is a puzzle. Preferences about depth and breadth of friends will no doubt be related to personality. For some people, all they really want is a significant other and a handful of close friends; others may like a wider range of friends and 'hobby buddies' plus lots of family members around them.

Physical activity likes

The more you enjoy the way you move your body, the more likely it is that you will both start moving in those ways and keep it up over the long term. Having an 'ideal' way to stay physically active advised by others is one thing – actually doing it is another. If the idea of going to a gym leaves you cold, then it is very unlikely you will do it on a regular basis. But if you love to walk outdoors or dance instead, then focus your activities around that. It is easier to add to or enrich a way you like to use your body to get added health benefits than to do something you really think you ought to do but dislike. Some people like to do physical activity alone; others like the support of doing it in a group. Some like it more formal and structured; others like it informal and ad hoc. Different body types may well prefer different types of physical activity – just the same as professional athletes who can vary enormously. A long-distance runner and a shot putter are so very different.

Arts and music likes

Music may have been thought about a lot more when we were teenagers – many of us had our favourite mixed tape which we spent ages putting together. In many ways, music is far more available these days with multiple devices and streaming capabilities. We can draw down all manner of music choices from the internet. (Ironically, younger people are taking to vinyl with much enthusiasm, like a new discovery.) It is easier than ever to experiment and try out new kinds of music.

If you were able to learn to play a musical instrument, which one most appeals and why? How much do you currently listen to music played on that instrument?

Making music with other people is increasingly popular, for example community choirs for those who like to sing. People often find that singing or playing with others gives them a sense of connectedness and satisfaction.

For broader arts, what sort of free tickets would you most like to receive? What sorts of activities would make you want to put a red ring around an advert, or write it in your diary? Who do you most enjoy going with – and how much are you happy to go alone?

Science interests

You don't need a formal education in science in order to have an interest in it. Which parts of science and the natural world do you find most fascinating? Where do you think science ends and the arts begin? Which sort of science and natural world programmes are you most likely to watch on TV? If you could sit round a dinner table with five scientists from the past or present, who would they be? What might you like to ask them?

Spiritual choices

As people age, the bigger questions in life can feel more immediate; for example, what is it all about, is there a higher power, what will happen to me when I die? What sort of questions would you most want to ask and how would you like them to be answered? Who would you most want to discuss them with?

Belief and doctrine can bring people together or drive them apart, depending on how they approach it. Being curious about this helps – openness and respect for difference can make one's relationship to the spiritual side of life much richer.

Action

One way of exploring this area is using a method first described by Kurt Lewin, a business psychologist: the forcefield analysis. It sounds a bit technical, but it is actually a very simple approach to understand what to do to get what one wants. In this case, what we want is 'to be myself', or a more specific part of being myself, for example, doing more creative things regularly.

Using this method, we map out everything we can think of that *helps us achieve* what we want (the so-called driving forces) and everything we can think of that is *getting in the way* of achieving what we want (the so-called resisting forces).

Examples of categories of driving forces (which are a combination of personal and external factors) are:

- my own skills/knowledge
- my own empowering beliefs and attitudes
- information I have or can get
- resources I have (e.g. money, space, time)
- people who will help me or will also benefit themselves
- physical abilities and health
- my own motivation

Examples of categories of resisting forces are generally the same as the driving forces, but the lack of them or the negative version:

- lack of knowledge/skills
- disempowering beliefs and attitudes
- lack of information
- lack of people who will help me
- people who will oppose me or not support me
- lack of specific resources

Method:

1   Get a large sheet of paper, preferably turned landscape. At the top right-hand corner, draw a circle and write in it what you specifically want to achieve or be.
    Then draw a diagonal line across the page, from top left to bottom right.

2   On the left side of the line, put in all the driving forces each with an arrow facing towards the circle.

3   On the right side of the line, put in all the resisting forces that are getting in the way, with arrows facing the other way, away from the circle.

4   Then consider carefully: what is likely to be the most powerful resisting force?
    What is the *first thing you can do* to start dealing with that?

Mapping it out this way will help you to see why you may be struggling with certain things that you want to do and be. It enables you to prioritise and find a place to start to constructively take action to get what you want. Because it is taking account of present realities in your life (and in your mind), it can help stop the endless daydreaming, wishing and hoping – and replace it with some constructive action instead.

Personality development

Our personalities can (and usually do) continue to develop throughout our lives. In this section, we outline a widely used theory of personality and personality development: psychological type or preference theory as proposed by Carl Jung and developed by Isabel Myers. This theory can help us make peace with ourselves, appreciate people with very different personalities and suggest where and how we may choose to develop our own personalities.

First, we outline the central idea of preference and its application to personality development when getting old. Other applications of preference theory included in this book are in Chapter 2, where we applied the theory (without naming it) to eating less, in Chapter 8 to sexuality and in Chapter 11 to some difficulties in communication and strategies for managing or resolving them, managing stress and making decisions.

The concept of preference

Preferences are certain personality characteristics which each of us feels are us at our most natural and comfortable, whereas others feel that the opposite characteristic is most natural for them. For example, if you prefer Introversion to Extraversion you will, given normal development and the opportunities, behave introvertedly most of the time and extravertedly some of the time, and Introversion will feel (and be) more comfortable and natural to you. For people with a preference for Extraversion, the opposite is the case.

The concept of preference is illustrated well by writing your signature, first as you usually do and then with your other hand. What is different about the two actions? Using your preferred hand usually feels more comfortable, natural and easy while the non-preferred hand feels awkward, clumsy and child-like. Moreover, while we can use our non-preferred hand, it takes more concentration and effort and is therefore more tiring and harder to sustain.

In traditional preference theory, there are eight preferences, arranged in four opposite pairs, for example Extraversion and Introversion. The preferences are described in the next section.

Both our preferences and our non-preferences usually develop throughout our lives, and the theory is optimistic about people in general developing their preferences most and 'being themselves' in this sense. However, some people develop one or more of their non-preferences most – like a left-handed person taught to be right-handed – and according to the theory usually don't 'feel right'. When this happens, they can develop their preferences and become more themselves. This happens to some extent naturally but can also happen deliberately, as suggested later in this chapter.

Brief descriptions of the eight preferences in current preference theory

The following descriptions can be used to investigate your own preferences if you wish. If so, please choose in a *provisional* way, behaving like a good detective. Your aim is to isolate your basic enduring preferences from other influences on your behaviour; these 'other influences' include culture, upbringing, roles, other personality characteristics, stress, self-image and how developed your preferences and non-preferences are, hence the need to gather clues and interpret them carefully and respectfully. This may sound like a formidable task, but in everyday life people are generally quite accurate in their judgements of their own preferences and those of others.

Some of the standard terms for each preference are indicated in the following, but please note that their names have a particular, technical meaning, so that, for example, Thinking does *not* mean 'without feelings', and Judging does *not* mean judgemental.

A summary of the preferences and some general characteristics associated with them is:

> Extraversion – More outgoing and active versus its opposite of Introversion
> Introversion – More reflective and reserved
> Sensing – More practical and interested in facts and details versus its opposite of Intuition
> Intuition – More interested in possibilities and overviews
> Thinking – More logical and reasoned versus its opposite of Feeling
> Feeling – More agreeable and appreciative
> Judging – More planning and coming to conclusions versus its opposite of Perceiving
> Perceiving – More easy-going and flexible

There are many ways of discovering or clarifying your preferences, including reading descriptions of the combinations of preferences; asking someone who knows you well to judge the accuracy of your choices; and observing your comfort with and energy for various ways of behaving. The results of the free questionnaire and scoring at Keirsey.com provide a useful clue to preferences.

If you don't find a good enough best fit between the various clues and your own or another person's personality, it may mean that the theory or parts of it don't apply to you or that you need more time to clarify your or their preferences. For example, X saw himself as preferring Introversion, Intuition, Thinking and Judging, but his closest friend at the time, who knew him well, said that X really preferred Feeling and Perceiving. X disagreed and left it there for over a year.

This error (as it turned out to be) is partly explained by his being so pleased with the Introvert and Intuition descriptions that he took it for granted that his other two choices were accurate too. During the year, he observed his behaviour and feelings about them more carefully and critically. He said to one of his students (who preferred Judging and who said she thought he didn't) that his enjoying marking which TV programmes to watch in the weekly schedule was a clue for Judging. Her sceptical expression and his observation that he treated the marked schedule very flexibly were useful clues for both Feeling (enjoying making decisions about what he liked) and Perceiving (some planning, but very flexibly).

X also read more about the preferences and saw more people with various preferences in action, and gradually realised that, although his Thinking was quite developed, his Feeling was 'more him', and as for Judging, it was not very developed (so far, and nothing like as much as his Perceiving). How could he ever have misjudged his personality so much?

This example illustrates some of the complexities of clarifying one's preferences (and therefore non-preferences). However, although such judgements should be provisional, they are usually made – accurately – much more quickly than X made his.

Preference theory is useful for understanding and improving personality development in later life in two ways. The first applies to normal development in which our preferences develop first and much more naturally and easily than our non-preferences, as befits core characteristics. However, in later life we put more emphasis on developing our non-preferences (though not developing them as much as our preferences).

The second, more unusual development path is that some of us develop one or more of our non-preferences first, because of the way we were brought up. For example, X, who prefers Feeling, is brought up to see this preference as not manly and therefore sees himself as preferring Thinking. He feels uneasy or uncomfortable about this sometimes. Two main possibilities for him are 1) to continue to ignore the impulses to express and develop Feeling and never find his true self in this respect or 2), perhaps through a relationship or counselling, to notice, value and develop his Feeling. He will then feel more fulfilled and be more effective.

Some ways of developing each preference and non-preference are:

For Extraversion	• Be spontaneous
	• Speak to an audience
	• Speak to someone you don't know
For Introversion	• Be alone for longer than usual for you
	• Listen when you'd rather speak
	• Read quietly for longer than usual for you
For Sensing	• Observe and keep observing (an exercise prominent in mindfulness)
	• Be very specific about something
	• Focus on someone's actual words and how they speak, including gestures and changes in tone
For Intuition	• Brainstorm
	• Give an overview
	• Focus on possible underlying meanings of what someone is saying and not saying
For Thinking	• Create a flow chart
	• Do a cost-benefit analysis for a decision
	• Define something precisely
For Feeling	• Clarify your values
	• Give a compliment
	• Reflect on what matters most to someone you know well
For Judging	• Make a list of things to do, do them and tick each one off as you finish it
	• Resist an impulse
For Perceiving	• Act on an impulse
	• Re-examine a decision and gather more information which may be relevant to it
	• Relax instead of completing or finishing something

The following steps are an approach to developing your preferences and non-preferences:

Step one – consider how developed each of your preferences is in the way outlined earlier, e.g. like a good detective

Step two – consider how developed each of your non-preferences is

Step three – consider whether you want to develop any of your preferences or non-preferences further and choose one to focus on

Step four – choose from the ways of expressing that preference or non-preference and decide how to behave more in that way

Step five – observe carefully your experience and evaluate it

Usually, when part of your real self is waiting and ready to be developed, the process is enjoyable: it feels very right. But occasionally the corresponding non-preference has been so thoroughly practised and the preference so thoroughly discouraged that it can be more of a struggle: it can feel squashed and submerged. This complexity tends to happen in later life when there is more time for reflection and less authentic ways of behaving are more ingrained.

Identifying core motives

This section describes two approaches to identifying the core motives in temperament theory and three variations of the Strivings Assessment Questionnaire (SAQ), which is much more focused on individuality in motivation.

Temperament theory I

Temperament theory is a variation of preference theory that suggests that four combinations of some of the preferences are particularly powerful for understanding behaviour: Sensing plus Perceiving, Sensing plus Judging, Intuition plus Thinking and Intuition plus Feeling. The assumption is that one temperament is dominant in each of us. Linda Berens in her booklet *Understanding Yourself and Others: An Introduction to Temperament* expressed this idea dramatically. She wrote that blocking it is like 'psychological death', and that people feel 'light of spirit' when their core motives are met and 'drained of energy' when they are not.

A version of the motives at the core of each temperament is listed next. Which is most like the real you? Which next most? And so on. Alternatively, you may like to try choosing the one *least* like you first and then the one you could not live without. The outcome may be, for example, the combination of Intuition plus Feeling as most like you, with Sensing plus Judging hardly at all.

Examples of core motives in the four temperaments are:

Sensing plus Perceiving (SP) Solving practical problems quickly, expediently and with flair; being free
Sensing plus Judging (SJ) Being responsible and useful to a group or community and planning in detail

Intuition plus Thinking (NT) Designing new theories and models and analysing intricate problems with precision; being competent

Intuition plus Feeling (NF) Developing an authentic identity, helping other people to do the same; harmony and finding something worth believing in

The following observation by Otto Kroeger and Janet Thuesen in *Type Talk* illustrates temperament theory well. They were writing about the way their guests behave around their swimming pool:

- Our SP guests always grab all the pool toys, head right for the water and invent a new game.
- The NFs spread on the lounge chairs and talk earnestly about life and people.
- The NTs dangle their feet in the water, rib each other and critique the issues and people in their professions.
- And the SJs always, always find some work to do, like hanging up towels, husking corn, scrubbing the grill or pulling weeds from the garden.

Temperament theory 2

Another approach to clarifying core motives is to work from the specific to the general by thinking about one or more of the most fulfilling or enjoyable projects you've ever worked on. Then, consider which if any of the needs associated with the temperaments fits your chosen projects best.

Personal strivings

Personal strivings are what we typically try to do or want to try to do in our everyday behaviour. A simple questionnaire is used to explore them: the Strivings Assessment Questionnaire (SAQ). It asks you to complete the sentence stem 'I typically try to . . .' several times (say 10–15 times). Next, rate each personal striving, for example using a 1- to 6-point scale (where 6 is high) and these three criteria:

- how committed you are to each striving;
- how rewarding you find it; and
- how difficult you find it.

Another criterion, with a hint of Linda Berens' phrase 'psychological death' when she was discussing the power of core motives in temperament theory, is to ask, 'how *essential* is it for you?'

The aim of the SAQ is to reveal how a person thinks about their goals and therefore indicate their core motives, clarify them and at some point perhaps challenge them, e.g. with how well they fit with developing preferences/non-preferences or whether they are likely to be achieved or not.

Here is an example of responses to an SAQ:

1   Become more extraverted – less timid with the people I know
2   Not be dominated (bullied?) by H
3   Take more pleasure in everyday small things
4   Eat less chocolate
5   Answer my emails more quickly
6   Re-read all of X's books
7   Help my sisters more
8   End with my scary counsellor
9   Phone my parents once a week, at least
10 Take more pleasure in everyday things

SAQ 2

Step 1

Very quickly, write 100 statements completing the stem 'I want . . .'. Repetition is allowed.

Step 2

Analyse the activity and particularly the 100 statements. Did you answer freely? Are any wants repeated? Are any surprising? Are any enlightening? What do they tell you about your motives?

SAQ 3

The final method is another variation of the SAQ and is more elaborate:

Step 1

Write a list of all the things you'd like to have but don't have at present – anything at all, including feelings and possessions. No time limit: take as long as you like to write the list.

Step 2

Prioritise each item on the list as most desired, next most desired and so on.

Step 3

Explore how each of the top-rated items, say the top five, would change your life if you achieved it. What difference would it make?

Step 4

What motives seem most prominent? How much do they feel as if they're from you? This is a key step for uncovering possible core motives.

Step 5

Do you still want the items on the list as much as when you rated them as most desirable, etc.?

Step 6

Choose one item, brainstorm possible ways of moving towards achieving it and devise an action plan.

Identifying strengths

The concept of strengths has been revived and refreshed by Alex Linley in his book *Average to A+. Realising Strengths in Yourself and Others*. Linley's carefully expressed definition of a strength is 'a pre-existing capacity for a particular way of behaving, thinking, or feeling that is authentic and energising to the user, and enables optimal functioning, development and performance'. Some key points about this definition are that our strengths are inside us, either at birth or developed as children; when we use our strengths, we feel more real, fulfilled and energised; doing something well isn't the same as enjoying it, though there is some overlap; and a very important point: everyone has some strengths.

Many questions are raised by Linley's definition: 'So we can't be anything we want to be?', 'Some strengths are genetic and some learned?', 'How can I discover what my strengths are?' and, more subtly, 'Is it possible to overuse a strength?' and 'Is it true – it's such a romantic idea – that our strengths, or some of them, can be hidden from us?'

An example of a strength is Lift – improving the mood of others through being optimistic and encouraging. Another is Bounceback – using setbacks to achieve more than you expected. Other terms for strengths are more familiar – e.g. Curiosity, Kindness, Humility. If your reaction to Lift, Bounceback etc. is to feel inadequate or despairing, that is not the intended effect of a strengths-based approach! Rather, the idea is to feel encouraged to look for our own strengths.

The orthodox approach to identifying our strengths, and often a good starting point, is to complete a questionnaire. Free questionnaires, scoring and interpretation are available at www.viastrengths.org and www.authentichappiness.org. New developments will be reported on the Centre for Applied Positive Psychology (CAPP) website, www.cappeu.org. A limitation of the questionnaires is that there may well be many strengths which haven't been named yet.

Another option is to take part in an Individual Strengths Assessment (ISA), developed at CAPP, with a specialist interviewer or coach. The underlying method accepts that asking someone or oneself directly 'What are your strengths?' may be too abstract. Rather, questions like 'Tell me about a really good day for you', 'When do you feel most alive?' and 'What sorts of activities give you the most energy?' are asked as part of a conversation. A supplementary and minor strategy in the ISA is to ask about activities that are weaknesses or are draining. The replies are carefully observed for clues, and the clues noted for later feedback. They may also be followed up at the time, looking for further evidence for or against a real strength.

Other strategies are to:

- notice what you really look forward to doing
- notice what 'comes easily' to you, with the proviso that some people take one or more of their strengths for granted
- notice what you miss doing
- explore your memories of early childhood and ask others about you then: what themes and patterns can you identify, and how are they related to your current experience and behaviour? Linley uses the concept of a 'golden seed' – when someone remarks on an ability or talent in us and we remember the remark; teachers, relatives and guardians or parents are all likely sources (as they are of 'leaden seeds')

- explore who you admire and why (it may be easier to see some of your own strengths in someone else)
- ask other people who know you well when you're most energised and when you're at your best
- if you know your preferences, read the descriptions of them for strengths that are characteristic, and see if they apply to you and if you want to develop them further

Identifying values

Personal values tend to stay implicit for most people. Few people actively and overtly set out their values or articulate them to others. In contrast, many businesses and organisations have mission statements and values statements up front on their websites and documents, in the belief that people need to know what drives them and what they stand for.

People may be more familiar with the cultural or religious value system which they are a part of. These may be easier to understand as they are often articulated more and can be seen to be shared by many people. Personal values, however, are less obvious, but we all have them as individuals. They are quietly acting as drivers, motivators or avoiders underneath, often without the person knowing about it. Sometimes people only know what they value when it is threatened, walked over or ignored. Generally, we only get really worked up about something if it is really important to us.

This is the nub of personal values – they are usually abstract nouns that describe what really matters for us. For example, for some people it could be security, obedience and loyalty; for others adventure, exploration and freedom will be more important. They are not just superficial, changeable preferences or desires – they are deeply held ways of being that are centrally important to who we feel we are as a human. If we had to write our own personal 'mission statement' in life, our values would be central to it.

Although most lists of values are abstract nouns, for some people it is easier to see something more concrete as a value. For example, owning a particular house might be a (or the) top core value for someone who doesn't want to include it within another value, like security, escape from 'normal life', environmental friendliness, status, etc. Generally, though, it is clearer to work through to greater abstractness.

This may seem a bit philosophical and theoretical to some people, but values are very useful to get familiar with in many practical areas of our lives. Living congruently, in line with what is really important to us, is a recipe for personal peace and happiness. However, living in a way that is at odds with our values can spell itchy discontentment at best and misery at worst.

One of the interesting things about personal values is that they may surprise others. It can be tempting to make assumptions about other people's values, perhaps thinking they will coincide with your own or the predominant cultural values. This is as potentially foolish as assuming someone else shares the same political views – and we all know how embarrassing or irritating it is being at a social event with others who assume you voted the same way they did.

There are three difficult issues that can arise concerning values.

The first, most obviously, is not being aware of them and not knowing why the choices you are making aren't working. Something simply doesn't feel right, and you can't quite put your finger on why.

The second is thinking you can just get a grip and get on with something (that, unbeknownst to you, is not congruent with your values) and it will all be okay if you just try a bit harder. Obviously, we all have to do things in life that we may not particularly like now and again, but it becomes a serious issue if we sign up to long-term situations that are not congruent with our values. Clarity about your values makes being assertive (e.g. saying 'no') and making decisions more straightforward.

The third is when we are in a close relationship with another, like a spouse, and there are two sets of values to be taken into consideration in all the important decisions you inevitably have to make as a couple. Knowing each other's values can aid important negotiations, as these can be overtly put on the table and worked with respectfully.

Clarifying values

There are a number of ways of getting clear about what your values are and different methods appeal to different people.

Method 1

This looks at important areas of your life and asks questions about them, looking for the underlying reasons why they are important.

The areas of your life can be:

* relationships
* work
* leisure
* health
* money
* environment
* other areas (such as religion/spirituality)

For each area, ask yourself these questions, and jot down the words that come up (or ask someone you trust to work with you on this):

* What do I value about . . . (e.g. my relationship with my husband)?
* What is important to me about . . . ?
* What do I get out of . . . ?
* What else does it give me?

Method 2

A direct approach to discovering your core values is first to ask yourself, 'What really matters to me?' and, perhaps separately, 'What really doesn't matter to me?', and to make two lists. Single words or brief phrases may be most useful. The second step is to decide which values are your top and bottom priorities, aiming for five or so in each set. This may not be a quick process, and you may wish to refine your choices as your awareness deepens, or as you or your life change. A further perspective is to examine the origins of each value, as a way of checking its real importance to you.

Method 3

Emotions are good clues to values. For example, if you groan whenever Manchester United are mentioned positively, this suggests a low value for that team or for football in general or for aspects of English Premier League football. The 'whenever' is important: values are usually defined as enduring beliefs about what matters to you and what doesn't matter.

Another useful clue from emotions is to notice your emotional reaction to things that really upset you. The strong emotions may be a clue to something that is very important to you being rubbished or transgressed. This may be a more 'working it out backwards' method, but sometimes we only know what is really important to us when it is taken away or threatened in some way. So, for example, if someone is very upset by the meanness and tightness of others, then it may suggest that generosity is an important value to them.

Prioritising values

You may find out you value, say, 10 main things in life. For example, they could be achievement, security, honesty, dependability, fairness, respect, commitment, independence, wealth and learning. However, it is even more useful to know which of those 10 you value the most. So they need to be prioritised from 1 to 10.

There are different ways of prioritising values. The first is to put your list on sticky notes in a line and re-order them with the most important on the top.

Another way is to make forced paired choices, so you consider each value in relation to each of the others in turn and ask yourself 'of the two, if I could only keep one, which one would I keep?' Give a tick to the value that you choose in each comparison, add the ticks up at the end, and re-order the list of values according to which gets the most ticks. Lindsay West describes this in more detail in her book *Coaching with Values*.

Different types of values in specific situations

There are other situations where it is useful to be explicit about what we value when making a particular decision, for example moving house. Most people have a list of moving criteria that they want to satisfy, regarding where they live and the sort of home it is.

Take time to really think about what is important to you regarding where you live. It is such a big and expensive decision that you will want to avoid making a mistake (as far as possible). You can link this to your general underlying values. It may be something that is fairly specific, like living in a certain area of the country or having enough bedrooms to accommodate family gatherings – or it could be more general, like somewhere where there is peace and quiet or where there is easy access to nature (because peacefulness and nature are two of your personal values).

Try and come up with a list of about 10–15 moving home values/wants. For example, it could include a large garden/within 15 minutes' drive to a train station to the city/where there is a lively social and cultural scene within walking distance/old cottage style/place for parking two cars/a view from the reception room window/within 30 minutes' drive to the coast/easy access for friends and family to visit. See how much your home values and wants correspond with or reflect your personal values. So if you really value going to live theatre, for example, how will you do that if you live in a rural area with no theatres within easy reach?

By doing the prioritisation of the home values/wants, you can clearly see which aspects you might possibly be willing to compromise on in order to achieve the more important values. You will note that some options you were previously considering become eliminated as they do not allow your most important values/wants to be fulfilled. This is particularly important when there is more than one person making the decision – in this case, two (or more) sets of values need to be worked on, and you can't assume that your lists of values will be the same. Even if they were, once they were prioritised, the order of importance would most likely be different. Moving to a home where only the values/wants that appear at the bottom of your prioritised list get met (and the most important ones don't) will probably cause problems in the long run.

Example:

Value no.	Home value/want	Scoring
1	Large garden	√√
2	Within 15 minutes' drive to a train station serving the city	√√√
3	Lively social and cultural scene within walking distance	√√√√√√√
4	Old cottage style	√
5	Place for parking two cars	√√√√
6	View from the reception room window	√√√√√√
7	Within 30 minutes' drive to the coast	√√√√√√√√
8	Easy access for friends and family to visit	√√
9	Detached house	√√√√
10	Quiet road	√√√√√√

Chapter 8

Relationships

.

In this chapter we look at selected aspects of relationships. We start with a discussion about online dating, styles of romantic love, personality and sexual behaviour and coping with sexual problems. We then turn to the issue of loneliness and what we might be able to do about it. Finally, we have included a short section on owning pets as they frequently provide a daily source of relatedness, especially if we live alone.

Online dating

Online dating is a contemporary solution to the problem of getting enough human interaction. This is most likely to appeal to you if you want a fling or romantic love (variously defined), but can on occasion lead to a new acquaintance or friendship. Attitudes to online dating have changed dramatically, from it being seen as shameful and desperate to gaining wide acceptance.

Online dating has great potential for good, but there are also risks and problems. The most positive aspect for many people is the huge number and variety of people there are to choose from or be chosen by. The risks include security, rejections and becoming unkind – there are always more 'candidates' to assess and reject, and they can become dehumanised in the eyes of the person rejecting them.

To make good choices of who to meet or invite to meet, it may be useful to know what qualities in a partner are most important to you. You may like to try listing your top three. Of course, the more qualities you list, the less likely you are to find all or most of them in one person. Also, you may, because of your lovestyle (described later in this section), see this exercise as pointless or irrelevant to finding true love.

If you also want to increase your chances of being chosen by people you would choose and not to sabotage your chances if you meet, we suggest using a recent photo that does you justice but no more than that, and writing a succinct, specific and accurate profile.

The process of online dating is usually first to exchange a few messages online or on the phone, then if it seems to be going well, one of you will suggest meeting. If you both agree to meet, then a coffee or drink have the advantages of being relatively easy to end if, for example, the person's photo is of a much younger them and that matters to you. On the date itself, we hope you will try to make a balance between listening – including questions you ask the other person which relate to something they've said and leaving space for them to speak – and speaking about aspects of yourself.

It may also help to be prepared for – even to expect – disappointment. Probably the most likely outcome is a mutual agreement that it was good to meet but not to meet again – quite liking each other, but no 'chemistry'. There is a real skill in ending such meetings well, but it is reported to be not widely used. Instead, there is 'ghosting', which is simply not replying to emails or other attempts at contact. The alternative and probably often neglected skill is to be honest with yourself and then with the other person, respecting their feelings and being ready to deal with a variety of reactions such as anger, embarrassment, sadness and relief. The section on assertiveness skills in Chapter 11 includes some relevant ideas and details of the skill of saying no.

You may find it helpful to keep a journal or diary after each meeting. How did you feel before, during and after the meeting? Excited, flat, drained, interested? Were you particularly happy or mortified about anything they or you said or did? Are there any implications for how you are with the next person you meet or the next time you meet this one? Hopefully your notes will not be needed for long before you meet somebody who appeals enough (or more) and who feels the same way about you.

A subtle problem with online dating is that it can seem the only way to meet a desirable partner when, in fact, relationships still begin in other ways. Indeed, many romantic relationships do not start online. Another subtle problem, touched on earlier, is that treating other people as easily disposable can leave you feeling shallow.

There are numerous and very varied dating websites, and it's a matter of researching them online or through asking people who've tried them to find those that are most likely to suit you.

Romantic love: Lee's theory of lovestyles

John Lee's ideas about styles of loving can be a helpful perspective on worries or puzzles about true love. They can also be challenging or threatening to a particular relationship or to a belief about true love. Lee suggested five lovestyles plus three main combinations:

> Eros: Immediate physical attraction, delight in the other person, intense
> Ludus: Playful, free of commitment and deliberately avoids intensity
> Storge: Friendly, companionable and affectionate
> Pragma: Practical and realistic, a 'shopping list' style – arranged marriages and some approaches to internet dating
> Mania: Feverish, obsessive and jealous, intense
> Storgic Eros: Friendly intensity
> Ludic Eros: Playful intensity
> Storgic Ludus: Friendly playfulness

A major strength of Lee's model is that each style is true love for some people. If you are surprised by or recoil from one or more of them, it's probably a good clue for your own lovestyle or styles. Lee's theory also answers many questions about love, like 'Does real love appear suddenly or gradually?' and 'Do I really love X?' So, for example, part of the answer to whether true love appears suddenly or gradually is that it depends: in the Eros style, it's instant, and in Storge, it's gradual.

A complicating (but sometimes very welcome) aspect of Lee's theory of lovestyles is that while each of us has a preferred style of love, some people can love different partners in different styles or the same partner in different styles at different times. For example, quite a common pattern is changing, perhaps quite gradually, within the same relationship, from Eros to Storge, i.e. from intense to peaceful.

A risky but brave application of Lee's theory is to discuss your own and a partner's lovestyle with them. Lee's book *Lovestyles* is unfortunately out of print, but there are more details on the internet, including a questionnaire. Discussing some or all of the items of the questionnaire with a partner or potential partner is another level of analysis – and possibly riskier still – but bear in mind that Lee found good relationships in all combinations of his lovestyles!

Personality and sexual behaviour

The preference theory of personality explains, at least in part, some major differences in what people find erotic or a turn-off, and it does so without seeing the differences as unnatural or one of them as superior to the other. It suggests that some people really are mismatched, but it is also true that we vary in how flexible and adaptable we can be or want to be.

The preferences for Extraversion etc. can be associated with various sexual behaviours which follow directly from the theory:

- people who prefer Extraversion like to talk during sex and to be direct about their reactions and feelings, while Introverts don't talk much or at all during sex
- people who prefer Sensing tend to 'stay present, stay physical', while those who prefer Intuition talk more broadly
- people who prefer Thinking like to work on improving their skills and techniques, while those who prefer Feeling are more likely to emphasise romance and being in the mood
- people who prefer Judging like to give notice or have a routine, and those who prefer Perceiving like to be surprised

You may recognise some of these differences in yourself and others and smile. Or you may wish to treat some of them as ways of developing a preference or non-preference as discussed in Chapter 7. The sexual behaviours listed (and of course others) can also be discussed with the relevant partner, and sometimes their consistency with personality differences will make blame and conflict less likely. The other person is probably not setting out to disappoint you!

For example, Z's partner described the way he kissed her, with an affectionate but puzzled smile, as 'like kissing a corpse'. His version was that he likes gentle kissing and that she kissed like a Labrador (said warmly but sadly). They had then showed each other how they especially liked to be kissed and smiled ruefully about the huge difference, but it seemed like an unmovable gap and perhaps one that indicated deeper future problems for them as a couple. They also found that his preferring Introversion and her preferring Extraversion made their differences a bit easier to accept, and in some relationships it could potentially have done more, but for them it was not a solution, and she ended the relationship.

Coping with sexual problems

Many sexual problems can be resolved by discovering what you do and don't like sexually and finding someone who shares at least some of those preferences or is willing to experiment. His or her full informed consent is vital here and so is honest, clear discussion. Examples of solutions are avoiding penetrative sex, examining beliefs such as frequency being more important than quality or the opposite, that sex should always be sensational (as it tends to be in films), trying different positions, saying a particular word or phrase or deciding to be celibate.

If good communication between partners doesn't solve a sexual problem, modern medical treatments and counselling can be very effective; see your GP or the College of Sexual and Relationship Therapists (cosrt.org.uk).

Loneliness

There are some horrible truths about loneliness. It can enter by the back door, when one is not expecting it, and it can linger in a vague presence that is quietly life-sapping. It is alarmingly common and it is not good for health, mental or physical.

Fortunately, there is now increasing awareness of the prevalence of loneliness and of the negative impact it has on people's lives. In the UK, there are a number of initiatives that have been set up to understand and deal with loneliness. In October 2018, the UK government launched its strategy for tackling loneliness. This followed on from the campaign work that Jo Cox organised as an MP before she was murdered. A generally accepted definition of loneliness used by the Campaign to End Loneliness and the UK government strategy is 'a subjective, unwelcome feeling of lack or loss of companionship arising from a mismatch between the quality and quantity of the social relationships that we have and those that we want'.

It is recognised that it is not just a straightforward situation of not having enough social companionship. It is subtly linked to a range of other factors at the individual, family and society level. Isolation, health and ageing can play a part, as well as structures and cultures in society. It has been reported that more individualistic cultures that value independence (such as northern Europe and North America) are paying a price by experiencing increased loneliness. Cultures that are more inter-dependent (like southern Europe and South America) have denser social networks, where there are fewer people in an individual's network but they know each other better. These cultures tend to experience less loneliness.

The UK Office of National Statistics looked at what factors are present when people report being lonely – the most common characteristics are being widowed, having poor health, having a long-term illness or disability, having caring responsibilities and being unemployed. The other most common factor was being aged 16–24, so it is not just a problem of older people, despite the usual stereotypes.

The government is now looking at ways of defining and collecting more consistent data on the prevalence of loneliness. Recent survey estimates from the Office of National Statistics and from the Campaign to End Loneliness suggest that 5-18% of UK adults feel lonely often or always. There are an estimated 1,100,000 chronically lonely people aged 65 and over. Thirty percent of people aged over 80 reported being lonely in 2014–15. About 11% of people over 75 reported having no close friends in 2011–12. This is a serious public health issue, likened to the seriousness of smoking and obesity.

The effects of frequent or longstanding loneliness on health are often cited – it is associated with a number of health problems. These include increased risk of coronary heart disease and stroke, increased risk of cognitive decline and dementia, increased risk of depression, low self-esteem and sleep problems. It can also set up vicious circles whereby loneliness changes our perceptions, expectations and memories of our interactions with others. Looking through these grey-tinted spectacles, we think others are behaving in more unfriendly ways than they actually are, and this sets us up for withdrawal and more loneliness.

An added issue is the stigma associated with loneliness. It is estimated that about a third of people in Britain say they would be embarrassed to say they felt lonely. This is one of the things the government strategy wants to change – so that people are more open to seeing it as a normal phenomenon that may be the result of a number of factors stacking up and therefore not a character flaw or weakness. It has been the same story for mental health issues such as depression and anxiety. It may well help that people in the public eye are more willing these days to open up about their own personal experiences of mental health problems without feeling a sense of embarrassment or shame.

BBC Radio 4 undertook a large loneliness survey in 2018 before the government strategy was launched. They collaborated with academics and the Wellcome Collection and invited people to answer a large number of questions to do with their experience of loneliness, their health and wellbeing and their beliefs about loneliness and how to tackle it. There was a large response – 55,000 people aged between 16 and 99 answered, including 13,000 people aged over 60. Of course, this is a self-selected sample of people, so it may not necessarily be representative of the general population. However, there are some interesting results so far from this very large sample.

They found the people reporting to be the most lonely had issues with trusting others, and tended to have lower self-esteem and higher measures of neuroticism, although they didn't appear to have lower social skills. Interestingly, the lonelier people scored higher on empathy. Being a female carer was associated with a higher risk of loneliness. These are all associations and not necessarily causal – and it is not clear whether loneliness causes the related issue or whether it is the issue that makes one lonely, or a bit of both in a feedback cycle.

Managing loneliness

It is a good idea to view loneliness in terms of prevention and treatment, especially as one ages. When one realises how common loneliness is, it is wise to try to prevent it as best one can. It potentially links into so many factors in our lives, and viewing these with a preventive hat on must help. For example, when making choices about where to live, it would be sensible to consciously check for potential loneliness in the future, especially if there is a sudden change in one's circumstances, like a bereavement or illness that causes reduced mobility. Understandably, it has been found that loneliness is more likely in places where there is a lower sense of community. (See also Chapter 9, 'Deciding where to live'.)

Another preventive measure may be to review one's own social and relational 'resources'. If all of our relational eggs are in just one or two baskets, then it puts us in a precarious position, especially as we get older. Research suggests that single people tend to have wider social networks than married people and they are more used to having to spread their net more widely. One psychologist likens this situation to having a 'relational pension' – as it is not just money that needs to be put aside for our old age. We need to plan for enough social relationships too.

For people who are already lonely, there is a world of difference if this is a more fleeting, temporary feeling or whether it is long-standing and chronic. Despite the stigma of loneliness, it is a normal human reaction to feeling socially and relationally 'hungry'. Knowing there are things one can do to relieve it and knowing it won't last forever can be great comforts. Admitting it to oneself is the first step towards tackling it – and then looking for helpful ways of alleviating it.

The top five things to alleviate loneliness suggested by the people who responded to the Radio 4 questionnaire were:

1   Do activities that distract you or dedicate time to work, studies or hobbies
2   Join a social club or take up new activities or pastimes
3   Change your thinking to make it more positive
4   Start a conversation with anyone
5   Talk to friends and family about your feelings

These suggestions will appeal to people differently, and some may not help the chronically lonely. One of the things that lonely people need to be aware of is how the experience of loneliness can change how they view others. It can erode trust in others, and it is easy to misinterpret cues or responses from others, thinking they are more negative than they really are.

Lonely people can have high expectations for their relationships with others. It can be helpful to consciously lower these expectations and learn to be content with different degrees of depth of relating with different people. Joining a choir, for example, and hoping to meeting a new best friend may set the expectations too high. Another perspective might involve viewing one's social/relational 'cake' as having different ingredients provided by different people and different situations. It may be asking too much to expect to get the entire cake made from one or two people in older age, even if this has been your experience earlier in your life. Changing one's attitudes may be easier said than done, and some people may need support with this.

Personality type will no doubt have an effect. For example, people with preferences for Extraversion, Sensing and Perceiving may, in general, find it a lot easier to enjoy meeting different sets of people for sports or hands-on hobbies. Many Introverted, Intuitive types may prefer fewer, deeper relationships, and this puts them at a disadvantage if life events or circumstances lead to a change in their existing close relationships (bereavement, for example).

Using social media can help, but research is suggesting that people reporting loneliness tend to have higher relationship expectations than non-lonely people. People who aren't lonely use social media more as an adjunct to their social life – to find out information, for example, or to connect with people they already know.

In the government strategy on loneliness, there are recommendations for setting up 'social prescribing' via GP surgeries, so that patients who appear to be at risk of or are suffering from loneliness can be referred to various community support schemes to help tackle it. Ultimately the prevention and treatment of loneliness requires a 'loneliness lens' to be put in front of all aspects of society – housing, employment, education, community facilities, etc. – to see how both subtle and more overt factors are contributing to this problem.

For us as individuals, it may help to have our own personal strategy to both prevent loneliness as far as possible and to do everything we can to alleviate it if it becomes a more long-standing problem. Seeing it more as a life situational issue to deal with (rather than an intrinsic personal problem) can help get us into 'problem-solving mode' in order to tackle it more effectively.

Pets

The decision to have a pet is a weighing up of pros and cons and doing a fair amount of homework. If you already have a pet, there are a number of issues to consider as you get older.

The good that pets do

There is increasing evidence that pets can have a beneficial effect on their owners, both physically and psychologically. For example, stroking a cat or dog can be relaxing, de-stressing and lower blood pressure and heart rate.

Obvious benefits of more usual domestic pets, like a dog or cat, are the companionship they give, especially if one lives alone. Having another living creature to care for and be responsible for can give a sense of purpose and belonging. Walking into a home and being greeted by a friendly animal with a wagging tail is a delight for many people.

Having a dog that needs exercising is a good way of giving structure to the day and ensuring that you do go out and walk yourself, all year round. It also makes people more open to others – as people are far more likely to stop and greet the dog, especially if they have one themselves.

If moving to a new area, a dog is a great way of meeting new people. It is a safe way of breaking the ice in a relaxed, unpressurised way.

The practicalities

The costs

The costs of pet ownership need a careful estimation. It is not only the cost of buying a pet, but also the monthly cost of feeding and caring for the animal. The costs of buying popular breeds of dog or cat have gone up considerably in the last 20 years or so. Even cross-breed puppies can now cost thousands of pounds, especially the crosses that have become in vogue, like poodle crosses such as cockerpoos.

Of course, where to buy them needs researching properly, especially for puppies and kittens, in order to avoid unscrupulous breeders and sellers (who are attracted to this area because of the vast sums of money that can be made). Advice can be sought from animal welfare organisations and charities, such as the Kennel Club, the Cat Society and their breed clubs and societies. Given the number of cats and dogs in rescue centres, it is most sensible to look here first. They are likely to ask some serious vetting questions to assess the suitability of potential new owners and their homes.

Other costs to take into account are for vaccinations and vet bills, insurance and care services if you go away and need to pay for boarding or home stays.

Does it suit your lifestyle?

Domestic pets are a big responsibility and a tie. This is especially important if one doesn't have a convenient 'back-up service' to step in and look after them. Trips away, if the pet can't come, require proper planning to take account of pet care. Cats are somewhat easier than dogs as they are generally more independent – but they still need sufficient human interaction and freedom to express their natural selves.

There is plenty of information online from vets and animal behaviourists about which breed of dog is suitable for different living environments and lifestyles. Never be tempted to buy a cute-looking small puppy without seriously thinking about what it will grow into and what its space and exercise needs will be.

As the Dog's Trust advert says, 'A dog is for life, not just Christmas'. It is a commitment for 10–18 years, depending on the breed. In general, smaller breeds and cross-breeds live longer. It is therefore possible that the dog or cat will outlive you – and subsequent provisions for the animal need to be thought through. There are charities that can help older people who are having difficulty exercising their dogs – like the Cinnamon Trust in the UK. They can arrange for volunteers to be regular dog walkers.

Another issue is if circumstances change and you need to go into a care home or other assisted living arrangement. Not all homes will allow pets, despite their potential health benefits. Giving up a beloved pet at such a vulnerable stage in one's life can be a great wrench.

Bereavement

As pets age, they can become more dependent and their needs can get more complex. This can make it difficult to arrange care for them if you need to go away. When the time comes, you can be faced with the awful decision about euthanasia. It will of course be a matter of carefully weighing things up, and your vet will help with this. Ultimately, it is a judgement call for the owner. Not everyone can understand the depth of grief that an owner can go through at the loss of their beloved pet, especially if they were their sole long-term companion at home. Some people say they couldn't bear to go through all that again, but with time they are likely to see it differently.

Chapter 9

Deciding where to live

In this chapter, we discuss the issues involved in moving house when you get older. We also focus on two other aspects of living arrangements – first, living alone and second, moving to a care home. Of course, there are other options that older people can consider, such as sheltered accommodation, assisted living and retirement villages. There is some excellent advice and information on these options on the Age UK website and its related factsheets. We think it is wise to start thinking about the whole range of options earlier, when we still have time to think about and research what our best choices might be for later on, rather than waiting until we are pushed into a quick decision due to unforeseen changes in circumstances.

Moving house

Reasons for moving house

Some estate agents remember the '4 Ds' as common reasons for prospective vendors wanting to move – divorce, death, debt and downsizing. Current young people would probably laugh at the concept of downsizing, as current house prices mean that many of them can't afford to get on the housing ladder at all or, at best, can only afford a small studio flat.

For older people, who have benefitted from more favourable conditions for buying their own homes, there is a lot more choice. The English Housing Survey in 2017 showed that 74% of people aged 65 and over owned their own homes outright. This was up from 56% in 1993. For younger people, the trend is in the opposite direction, and many of them are still likely to be renting when they reach retirement age.

For older people, circumstances may push them into making a move (e.g. the first two of the 4 Ds), but for others they may wish to rethink their living arrangements to suit them better as they get older.

Downsizing

With families having grown up and left home, some couples wonder why they are still living in a family-sized house that requires maintenance, heating, cleaning, etc. Despite the comforts of familiarity, it doesn't feel quite right. It may also be the case that some people don't get any happier or content with living spaces over a certain size.

If they have children who are really struggling with their living costs, some orchestrate a downsizing and gift the difference to their children to either help them get a leg up on that elusive ladder or just give them a chunk of money to contribute towards their living and rental costs.

Location

Another reason for moving is that the location doesn't suit your needs anymore. Perhaps the main reasons for living there in the first place are no longer so important, e.g. access to a train station for commuting or good local schools. The area could be one that's not, for example, diverse enough, quiet enough or vibrant enough to suit your life now. It may be too far away from family and friends. See also the section later in this chapter on living alone and geographical location.

Accommodation

What may have been ideal in the past may be less appropriate now. Three floors and many flights of stairs can be seen as a good way to keep fit – or else a complete pain – as you age. A good question to ask is 'is this making my life easier or not?' There's something quite unsettling about knowing that your living accommodation is not working for you, and is not supporting you in your daily life. Rather than struggling with what doesn't work, think about what would work better for you now –your ideal accommodation blueprint.

Things to be aware of

The process of moving

Moving house is often very stressful. This may be particularly the case if it is decades since you last did it. However, the process has changed over the last 20 years with the introduction of online information from estate agents and lettings agents. It saves all the travelling round that we used to do to sign on with agents, not knowing what they had to offer.

The legal side of it is much the same in the UK as it always was, although it has been speeded up somewhat due to being able to email correspondence and forms and many of the searches now being done online.

It is worth familiarising yourself with the chain of events involved in moving, and there are books and online guides on this that are helpful. If selling and buying, it helps if the estate agent has a dedicated 'sales progressor' whose job it is to ensure the process is going smoothly and can liaise with all parties, especially if there is a long chain involved.

If you need mortgage funds, retirement income–linked mortgages are available, but the whole mortgage system has tightened up considerably since the recession in 2008. The amount of information the lending companies require now can feel like an invasion of privacy for some people who haven't mortgaged for a long time.

Realistic assessment of costs

People who have done building projects and refurbishments often say the actual cost is about double your initial ballpark estimate of time and money. It can be similar with moving house. There are many non-obvious costs involved, which stack up to make the final total much more than you might have bargained for. So, at the start, it is sensible to plan out a realistic itemised estimate of the whole moving project, including the estate agent's fees, the legal fees, stamp duty, surveys, removals and any re-decorating and updating of the new home. It amounts to a sizeable – and non-returnable – sum.

A major unknown at the start, if you are selling and buying, is how much you can sell your existing home for and therefore what you might be able to afford to buy. Reputable estate agents will give a realistic assessment of this based on your local market conditions and what similar properties have actually sold for recently. It is an inexact science though – all a house is worth is what someone is willing to pay for it at that time. Bringing you on board with them by doing so-called flattery pricing may look very promising up front but can waste time and possibly miss good, realistic sales earlier on.

Avoiding mistakes

No one wants to go through all the costs of moving (time, energy and financial costs) to find out too late that they haven't got what they really wanted. Going through an assessment of needs and preferences is more detailed than just how many bedrooms you want and how much outside space and whether it is modern or period style. What is it that you really want and need and don't want or no longer need? Think about this now and, say, in 10 years' time. Some might say they'll just move again when they get older or if they get less fit or mobile. This could be a major undertaking or burden at a time when you may be much less inclined to do it, plus it is all the moving costs again – so it worth trying to 'future proof' your current move as best you can.

Doing an assessment of 'moving criteria and values' is useful as it sets out your blueprint of what you really want and need. See Chapter 7 on a suggested way to do this. Doing the prioritisation exercise is important, especially if there are two of you with different sets of preferences and needs. It enables you to explicitly discuss and explore how to get most of your joint priorities met as a team, rather than two individuals fighting from their corners.

Do you really need to move at all?

Sometimes things aren't working for you in the accommodation, but other aspects of where you live, like location, are just fine. It can be useful to get some advice (perhaps from a professional architect or designer) who can see the bigger picture on options for staying put. Aspects that you have assumed cannot be changed may be able to be altered enough to make it work for you. It may not necessarily be big structural changes that are needed but a rearrangement of how you use the spaces available.

All of this would need to revolve around what you need now from your living space. Paying for someone to come up with fresh ideas may be money well spent if it avoids a much larger expenditure on moving house. We may get so entrenched in our habitual view of our space that it is difficult to see it any other way.

Options for people who are not home owners

High private rental costs and the lack of social housing in the UK are regular news items and major political issues. Market rates on rentals are so high in certain areas that it pushes some people into financial hardship and even homelessness. Although it is recognised that many young people are in the so-called Generation Rent, where they have little or no hope of ever buying a home, the problem is still there for a smaller, but significant, proportion of current older people.

Recent research by the UK homeless charity Shelter has shown that a large proportion of older, private renters are spending over half their income on rent, whereas 30% of income is generally considered as the maximum that is affordable, especially for people on lower incomes. This is a political-social issue and needs tackling at that level. For individuals affected (or potentially likely to be affected later on), it is nonetheless worth thinking of other ways of easing the problem and doing it as early as possible. It is understandable that people in this situation may think they have no choices as they are so constrained by circumstance, but some out-of-the-box thinking may be of help, including thinking through some more unusual ways of providing housing.

Living alone

As most people know, the number of older people living alone is increasing. Data from the Office of National Statistics in UK in 2019 showed that 21% of people 65 and over live alone and 42% of people over 75 do. Is this a problem and, if so, what can an individual do to help themselves?

Humans are, at our core, social animals – it is written into our DNA as a survival instinct from the earliest times when the odds of living another day were a lot worse than now. Those who lived and worked together in groups were more likely to survive. Our DNA has hardly changed, but in modern life it is clear that individuals do vary in their desire and capacity to spend time alone and live alone. Introverts, for example, tend to need and enjoy more time alone than extraverts do, but there are many exceptions, of course. There are many people who need a lot of 'alone time' but nonetheless want the comfort and advantages of knowing they are not alone under their roof all day and every day. It can be comforting to know that someone else is in the next room or that someone will be around to eat with and when you wake up in the morning.

There are many people who are quite content to live alone and who lead full and enjoyable lives – so what is it that makes the difference?

One important aspect is how we ended up living alone, whether it was something we actively chose or something that was circumstantially thrust upon us. For the former, living alone may be fine for certain periods of time and at certain stages of life. All this can change, however, and it is likely that living alone at 60 is a very different ball game than living alone at 80. Our needs and circumstances can change, sometimes quite dramatically, and it may be difficult to predict or even imagine that they will. The change from an active choice (where there might have been other reasonable options) to no choice and no obvious alternatives can be shocking.

For the group who have living alone suddenly thrust upon them, there are more hurdles to jump. Usually, it will be as a result of a life event, like death of a partner or a divorce. But other things can happen – I know an elderly, single woman who was suddenly thrust into living alone when her younger sister, who had lived with her for many years, rather suddenly got married and left.

This gives two major issues to deal with – bereavement or loss as well as the sudden plunge into solo living. Living alone for the first time in decades requires a massive adjustment. Many couples divide up their activities into who is responsible for what, and it can easily be taken for granted that 'I do this' and 'you do that'. The 'you do that' responsibilities may be an alien territory to navigate if you realise you have very little or no experience or knowledge of how to do it yourself.

Aside from the practical 'keeping the show on the road' responsibilities, there are the less overt companionship needs. Assuming the relationship was reasonably harmonious, the loss of the other can feel like a complete paradigm shift. There is suddenly no one to think about and talk to in your immediate environment – no one to ask or be asked, 'would you like a cup of tea?'

There is another group who somehow find themselves living alone without necessarily having chosen it – things just pan out that way. Many of them may have preferred to live with others, but due to, for example, the breakup of a relationship earlier in life or lack of suitable partners or co-habitees, they end up living alone. Other people may mistakenly assume they have actively chosen this way of living, but they, themselves, have to just get on with it as best they can, sometimes for decades. The current modern way of living is not very geared up for this, especially for people who are around 45–65. They don't quite fit with the younger people who are more used to house and flat sharing and yet not yet old enough to want to take on older 'retirement community' living arrangements. There needs to be some middle ground where it becomes more normal for people to think about a newer way of sharing/communal living.

People who live alone can experience a rather surprising lack of understanding from their non-solo friends and family. When people are so used to living with others under the same roof, often for decades, they have no real notion of what it might be like to be living alone again, day in and day out, especially as a retired, older person.

For whatever reason one has ended up living alone, there are certain factors that need considering to try to make it a more manageable and positive situation:

1   Ensuring you get enough human interaction/companionship in your day and week
2   Considering carefully where you live and trying to future-proof it
3   Thinking outside the box

Getting enough human interaction

Getting enough human interaction will of course depend on how much each individual decides is 'enough'. For those who reckon they don't need so much, it is worth being mindful of slipping into too little interaction, just out of habit, and not quite bothering to make an effort. People living alone, who don't have social interaction at home on tap, have to make more effort to go out and find their interactions, or reach out to people via electronic means. They may have to learn how to be pro-active in looking out for social opportunities and get used to making the first move.

There is some debate about what type of human interaction counts more. In this age of digital connectivity, it is extraordinary that one can chat to a daughter on the other side of the world via

Skype or some other platform. I know a 90-year-old man who is a keen user of Facebook and WhatsApp. Clearly, this is so much better than not having such facilities, but it is still not the same as being in the same room as another human being. There are certain subtle aspects of connectedness that happen much better in the flesh.

If circumstances have changed, for example, retirement from a busy job, then suddenly the ready-made interactions from work disappear out of the equation. It may have been a real pleasure to come home alone after a busy day at work, and it is surprising to realise how much work contributed to the meeting of our social needs. Sometimes it helps to get a regular part-time job, and it can be an adventure to do this in a completely new setting or field. Volunteering is another way to get out and connect with others, but it does need to be in an area that really does put you in contact with people – a friend of mine reminded me that working in a charity shop doesn't necessarily mean she meets many people, as she spends most of the time out the back doing admin or organising donations, and the only person she sees much of is the manager.

Where you live

Living in an old cottage down a single-track lane in the countryside may be appealing and enjoyable for a fit, older couple or even a person living alone while they work. All of that can change if circumstances suddenly change – retirement or bereavement, for example. Living alone and being geographically isolated can tip the balance into an unforeseen problem. It can make everything that much more difficult. Bothering to make an effort to go out to see people (or inviting them to you) can be a major hurdle. Not many people are keen on driving 15–20 miles round trip to go out on a dark, wet winter evening.

Social isolation can also be considered in terms of who you'd like to live amongst and what facilities and social opportunities there are locally. Living in a 'dormitory' village or town may simply not work if there are not enough people like you and not enough activities to go to that you'd enjoy.

Thinking outside the box

If living alone doesn't really work for you, it is worth considering some alternative strategies. It is possible for more unusual arrangements to be made if people are willing to take a risk and try something new. For example, there are ways of pooling resources among two or more friends and sharing a living space that could even be carved up into private and communal areas. Another option is taking in a lodger if there is enough room or if the existing space can be re-arranged/extended in some way. All the 'yes, buts' to these solutions would need to be thought through and a strategy developed for dealing with them as best one can. For example, think of the legal situation of having a shared bought home – who owns what and is responsible for what and what to do if one of you wants to exit the arrangement, etc.

Thinking only in terms of 'couples/families' living together versus 'solo living' is very limiting. The current younger generation of Millennials is already having to change all this out of economic necessity and the unreachability of rents and mortgages, especially in large cities.

Of course, there are various communal living retirement home options. These could be a perfect balance of retaining some independence and onsite support and social opportunities. They tend to be expensive, however, and therefore unaffordable for many people. If they are in a converted large building (like an old school or convent) or even newly built, the geographical setting needs to be considered, as it may be too remote. It may then make you dependent on a car to get out and about as public transport in more remote areas is often not frequent or there at all. The reality may not be all the smiles of good-looking older couples seen in the advertisements and brochures. People can behave quite territorially and in an entitled way when suddenly living together in such close proximity with shared communal spaces. A couple I know who moved to a converted school had to do some concerted 'peace negotiations' with a prickly, more elderly couple upstairs in order for the curt 'notes' left at the communal entrance to stop.

Doing your homework on these options is so important to find out the realities of daily life and to compare that to what matters most to you. It is definitely a good idea to bring in an assessment of your values into any big decisions that need making (see Chapter 7).

Care homes

Generally, it will be some form of crisis or rapid deterioration of health that causes people to go into a care home. The decision about whether someone is at a stage to need a care home will mainly be made by the nearest relatives alongside their doctors, as by that stage the elderly person may no longer be in a position to make a reasoned assessment. Frequently the reason that care is needed is because of cognitive decline or dementia, when it becomes unsafe to leave someone unattended in their own home for any length of time. They may be admitted from home or from a hospital stay, when it is not considered appropriate or safe to discharge them back home. A physical condition or event (like an infection or a fall) that needed treatment in a hospital can be the thing that exacerbates the decline.

Sometimes, if there is an elderly spouse, they may be simply no longer able to cope as the main carer and so a care home becomes the only feasible option. Even with maximum at-home care assistance from social services and community health teams, it is still difficult to care for someone at home if they really need supervision 24/7. Getting private live-in help or nursing care is not always feasible as it is expensive and there needs to be suitable accommodation available.

Given that the final decision is often out of your hands, it is a good idea to think about this before getting to that crisis point or that level of decline. It is a bit like wills – some people think it is negative and morbid to think about such things when they are still well. This may be fine for people who have cooperative and caring families, when they can rely on a partner or one of their adult children to make a decision in their best interests. For people who have no children or no partner, it is wise to think through eventualities and what your preferred strategy would be, early enough to be discussed with someone you trust.

Which care home to choose

Over the last few decades, most of the provision has moved to the private sector. The majority of the local authority-run homes have either closed or been privatised. Care homes have had a bad press – if there is a horror story about abuse of residents or gross mismanagement, it tends to hit the headlines. Of course, this is a skewed picture as it doesn't report on all the many care homes that manage to look after vulnerable people in a caring and competent way. It is both physically and psychologically demanding work and relies on empathetic and extremely patient staff, many of whom will be paid relatively little.

It is very difficult to make an assessment about a care home if this arena is new to you and if it is in a geographical area you are not familiar with. Getting recommendations from other local families is helpful. Local healthcare providers, like GPs, would be a useful source of information when choosing a care home, but they would be unlikely to be able to be drawn on the subject. There are Care Quality Commission assessments and reports done regularly on care homes, and these are worth looking at. Ultimately, making one's own assessment through visiting the care home in person is essential.

Funding of care home costs

Anyone who has not been directly involved in a close relative or friend's entry into a care home is usually shocked at how much they cost. Currently, in the UK, the average cost of a residential care home per week is about £600, which is £31,200 per year. There are, of course, regional variations in this, with the north generally cheaper than the south. If the care home also provides nursing care, then the costs are usually well over £800 per week (£41,600 pa).

For people seeking support from their local authority, they will have a care needs assessment done, and if this shows that a care home place is required, then the individual will be means-tested. This includes the financial asset of their home, if they own one. In practice, this means their home will need to be sold in order to fund care, assuming they were the only one living in it. The individual has to completely self-fund if they have assets over £23,250. The council can offer a deferred payment agreement if an individual's house has to be sold.

Only when the individual's funds get down to the nationally indicated threshold will their local council step in to fund their care home costs. Each local authority agrees a nominated amount that they will pay towards care costs per week. This sum is often a lot less than the amount charged to private funders and so begs the question, where does the shortfall come from? The answer to this is not clear, but media investigations suggest that the 'real' cost of care homes would be some point in between the cost charged to private funders and the cost charged to local authorities. What this therefore suggests is that the private funders are, in effect, subsidising the local authority-funded places. In the past, this may have been dealt with by moving the client into a local authority–run care home but, as mentioned earlier, most of these have now been privatised.

Another method of funding care is via an immediate needs annuity. By paying a very large premium up front, the company will undertake to pay all the care home fees until the person dies. These sums are worked out like any insurance scheme so that the odds are in favour of the insurance company making money overall (as they are a business, of course). It also puts the relatives in the difficult position of trying to make a 'guesstimate' of how long the older person is likely to live.

Getting financial advice

Whichever route is decided to fund care, it is wise to involve a recommended independent financial advisor as the sums one would be dealing with are so large and it can be daunting.

If funds are generated from the sale of a home, they need to be properly managed. With the current paltry rates of interest in deposit and cash savings accounts, it means that the capital will shrink relative to inflation. Of course, the alternatives do require investments in stocks and shares and bonds which are subject to some uncertainty, even for people who want to invest at the lowest level of risk.

Making a decision about an immediate needs annuity policy requires a lot of thought and so it is advisable to get some professional advice. If there are no children or legatees of the elderly person, then it may be an easier decision to make, as no one else is particularly affected by all or most of the elderly person's money being used up. Of course, it is their money to be spent on them, but some elderly people want to try to safeguard their money as much as they can so that they can leave some to their family or chosen beneficiaries after their death.

Chapter 10

End of life – death, grief and making plans

In this chapter, we take a positive approach to the end of life. First, we outline the idea of a 'good death', as proposed by Kathryn Mannix, and then discuss some ways of making good deaths more likely to happen. Examples are joining a death café, engaging a doula and referral to a hospice. We also summarise the case for and against assisted dying. Next we consider additional actions we can take to make the end of our life more thought out and consistent with our wishes and values. They are organising a power of attorney, making a will, making a living will and planning a funeral. Finally, we discuss an experience which for many of us happens more often as we get older: coping with bereavement in ourselves and others.

A good death

Kathryn Mannix's approach to a 'good death'

Contemplating and accepting that we will die is part of getting old, though rarely easy and often avoided, hence the subtitle of Kathryn Mannix's 2018 book *With the End in Mind: Dying, Death and Wisdom in an Age of Denial*. Mannix has a lot of relevant experience as a palliative care consultant in hospices and patients' homes. She has encountered thousands of deaths and formed clear ideas about what normal dying is like and how to describe it in a helpful way to people who are dying or involved with others who are dying. Her conclusion is that when we are dying 'there is usually little to fear and much to prepare for'. If true, this view is a very comforting one.

In preparing for a death, she matches the pace of the person dying or involved, e.g. as a relative or carer, and when it feels appropriate, she asks what worries them about dying. Usually she is able to reassure them. For example, the person may be very afraid of pain and the effects of being drugged on their mental capacity, and she describes how modern drugs can remove the pain but leave the dying person's mind clear. She tells patients whose pain relief is not straightforward that enough morphine to control the pain would also sedate them, and that there is a choice to be made.

Mannix also describes how people normally die: essentially a peaceful process in which we gradually feel less energetic and more tired and consequently sleep more. Then gradually, perhaps over a few weeks we sleep more deeply and in time slip into a coma, becoming unconscious, not just asleep, part of the time. Near the end we're often unconscious all the time and our breathing starts to change. Sometimes it's deep and slow, sometimes shallow and fast. Then, gently, it stops.

This natural and peaceful dying is in marked contrast to what many of us believe dying to be like – great pain, struggling to survive and deeply sad. This bleaker view of what death is like tends to reduce the chances of the open, clear communication which is at the heart of Mannix's idea of a good death. Far too often, she believes, we keep people who are dying alive and rush them into intensive care for a treatment that is aggressive and ignores their wishes. Her approach emphasises giving the dying person the opportunity to choose, in a calmer and more aware way, what they will do and what treatments they will have and not have.

Supporting a good death

Joining a death café

In death cafés, people who usually don't know each other talk about any aspect of death and dying that comes up. Apart from feeling liberating to most people who go, and useful in itself, this is also practice in talking about death which can make helpful conversations about death more likely with friends and relatives. Health professionals too can struggle to tell patients they are dying, perhaps because it seems like a failure on their and medicine's part.

Engaging a doula

Doulas provide physical, emotional and spiritual support to people who are dying. Their role depends on their client's wishes and early in their time with a client they write a care plan together. Some doulas charge a fee while others are volunteers. Generally, they are connected to charities and hospices. Details are available from the organisation Living Well, Dying Well at lwdwtraining.uk.

Referral to a hospice

Hospices are far from being places where people just go to die. They offer a wide range of positive and practical activities, from pain relief and physiotherapy to workshops in painting, singing and yoga for patients with various terminal illnesses, including heart and lung disease. Moreover, many of their patients are cared for in their own homes or as day patients.

Assisted dying: for and against

The following bald statement of the arguments does not make a distinction between assisted dying for people with a terminal illness and those who are healthy physically and mentally and are competent to decide that they want to die. We have tried to be objective in our statements.

Arguments *for* assisted dying include:

> Assisted dying has been legal in some countries and states, e.g. the Netherlands, Switzerland, California and Canada for many years, with safeguards to prevent its abuse. The effectiveness of the safeguards is disputed.
> It is a caring and merciful act respecting human dignity and the right to choose.
> Some terminal illnesses can't be made bearable in palliative care.
> Its availability improves the honesty and clarity of conversations about death.

Arguments *against* assisted dying include:

> Assisted dying is currently (2021) illegal in the UK.
> People with terminal illness (or with disabilities) may feel pressured to kill themselves in order not to be or feel like a burden.
> Some people who want to die, e.g. because they are clinically depressed, change their minds later.

The sanctity of life, as a religious or ethical principle, takes priority. It's not needed because patients can legally refuse treatments that are keeping them alive.

This list of arguments only touches on the complexity of assisted dying. Moreover, some of them apply to people who are not ill but who want to die, which is even more contentious than assisted dying for people who are terminally ill.

Making plans for the end of life

There is something rather sobering about making plans for our own deterioration or demise. It is an area many of us would rather not have to think about – we might prefer to bury our heads in the sand and distract ourselves elsewhere. However, the issues don't go away. They may instead have to be dealt with by default legal or medical processes or by passing the buck to your next of kin.

Most of us want to make sure we have our say in how our lives are run, especially in significant decisions about the big things in life. We would not want our thoughts, feelings, preferences and values ignored when deciding where to live, who to live with, what work to do or where to go on holiday, for example. So why would we suddenly not mind what happens to us when we become older and more vulnerable and are not able to make decisions in the usual way? The difference is that these latter decisions need to made in advance at a time when we are best resourced to make them.

Areas where previous planning can be both responsible and helpful are:

1   Planning for who will be responsible for your best interests if you become unwell or lose your mental capacity to make sound decisions and manage your life.

   • *Power of attorney*

2   Deciding which treatments you would want/not want if you became seriously unwell or at the end of life and are unable to make or communicate your decisions at that time.

   • *Advance decisions/advance statements/living wills*

3   Making a will.
4   Planning what sort of funeral you would like.

Power of attorney

Power of attorney is a legally recognised process whereby you can set up in advance a plan of who will take over responsibility for your affairs should you become unable to make the decisions yourself or manage certain areas of your life.

The idea is to set it up and register it when you still have capacity to decide, so that it is 'ready in the wings' to be activated if and when a time comes when you need it, i.e. when you are no longer able to look after your own affairs.

It is not about passing power to someone else to run your life against your will and preferences – it is set up by you, for your best interests and preferences, with people you trust becoming responsible at a time that you need them to.

There are two main types of power of attorney that can be set up now:

• a lasting power of attorney (LPA) for financial decisions
• a lasting power of attorney (LPA) for health and care decisions

Before 2007, the LPA for financial decisions was called an *enduring power of attorney*. There is also a third type – an *ordinary power of attorney*, which is set up to cover certain responsibilities for your finances should you need it while you are still mentally capable – for example, if you are temporarily unwell, in a hospital or travelling abroad.

LPA for financial decisions

This covers areas such as managing finances, bank accounts and investments as well as paying rent, mortgages, bills and selling your home. It is up to you to decide when you want this to start as you don't have to wait till you are lacking mental capacity. Mental capacity is centred on someone's ability to understand information related to a decision, to actually make decisions and communicate their decisions. It is set out in law in the 2005 Mental Capacity Act, so there are clear safeguards for making this assessment.

In setting up an LPA, you decide who you want to be your attorney, and there can be more than one. You decide which sorts of financial decisions you will allow them to make, so it is not all or nothing. You also decide if you want your attorneys (if you have more than one) to make all decisions jointly or whether they are also able to make them on their own (called 'severally').

The process in England and Wales is managed by a governmental executive agency called the Office of the Public Guardian. The government website (www.gov.uk) has all the information needed to find out about lasting power of attorney and how to make one, including downloadable forms. It can be done oneself for a small registration fee without having to involve a solicitor, although some people like to take some legal advice about it, particularly if their financial affairs are complicated. The LPA needs to also have the signature of a certificate provider who confirms that you understand what you are signing and are not in any way under pressure. This can be someone you know well (but not a family member), or else a professional like a doctor or solicitor. Once registered, the LPA will officially sit with the Office of the Public Guardian until it is needed to be used.

LPA for health and care decisions

This is set up in a similar way as the LPA for finances, except it is to appoint an attorney who can make decisions on more general aspects of your life, such as what medical care you have, where you live, what you eat, who you should have social contact with, etc. It also covers decisions about life-saving treatments.

This LPA can only be activated into use if you lose mental capacity. Regarding a health decision that can be covered by an advanced decision, if there is a similar decision set out in the LPA (e.g. a wish to refuse life-saving treatments in certain circumstances), then whichever was signed the most recently takes precedence. Therefore, the attorney has to stick to the wishes that are set out in a more recently signed advanced decision.

The situation of losing capacity before setting up a power of attorney

If you became unable to look after your own affairs and can't make decisions due to a lack of mental capacity, then there is a safety net, but it is a long-winded and more complicated one. Without a registered LPA, then the Court of Protection in England and Wales may become involved. There is an application process for the Court of Protection for whoever it is who needs to make decisions on your behalf. The court would decide if they are appropriate to be appointed as a *deputy* to make decisions for you on either property and finances or personal welfare issues, or both. The role of a deputy is similar to that of an attorney, and they have to do everything that is in your own best interests. The main issue here is that you are not the person who chooses your deputy, and the process of appointing one can take a long time and be a lot more expensive than agreeing to an LPA.

In the worst-case scenario where there is no one to step in and make decisions on your behalf (i.e. if there is no family member or friend to offer), then an *independent mental capacity advocate* (IMCA) must be instructed to protect your rights. This system for advocacy was set up under the Mental Capacity Act.

The ReSPECT form

ReSPECT stands for Recommended Summary Plan for Emergency Care and Treatment. It is a further option for recording how you would like and not like to be treated in a health emergency if you can't express your wishes at the time. The form is completed in discussion with your GP. Details can be obtained from your GP surgery or at www.respectprocess.org.uk.

Advanced decisions, advanced statements and living wills

The terminology can be a bit confusing here. An advanced decision is also known as an advanced decision to refuse treatment and is known more colloquially as a 'living will'. It is a legally binding document that sets out your decisions about what you do and don't want to happen treatment-wise should you become unable to make or convey decisions at the time.

An advanced statement is a list of your more general preferences about day-to-day living should you become incapable of deciding at the time. It is not legally binding, but it should be taken into account by people who are acting in your best interests.

Advanced decisions

The advantage of making an official advanced decision is that you can set out all your preferences about what healthcare you do or don't want and under what circumstances you would like to be kept alive. It is set up when you are able to make decisions and must be signed by a witness if you decide you do not want life-saving treatment. Planning in this way is taking serious responsibility for deciding what is right for you – everyone is different and there is nothing right or wrong about one's preferences. It is an effective and legally binding process, whereas casually saying things like 'if ever I get like that, I want you to shoot me' (as one of our relatives used to say) is neither helpful nor legal.

An advanced decision needs to be specific about which treatments you are refusing and under what circumstances. To make it easier to write, there are suggested formats for writing one on charity websites such as Compassion in Dying (www.compassionindy ing.org.uk). Once it is done, it is not written in stone, as you can change your mind at any time and re-write a new one. Of course, you would need to let the relevant people know about it and where to find it written down, such as family members, your doctor or healthcare workers. It is a good idea to ask your doctor to keep a copy in your medical records.

There are various types of life-sustaining treatment that you are able to refuse, such as ventilation (if you can't breathe by yourself), antibiotics or cardiopulmonary resuscitation (CPR, if your heart stops). However, there are certain basic nursing care elements that cannot be refused in an advanced decision, such as pain relief, food and drink and basic nursing to keep people warm and comfortable. It is not possible to demand certain treatments that healthcare staff do not think are clinically appropriate. As the current law stands in the UK, it is not legal to ask for euthanasia or to have someone assist you in taking your own life, so this cannot be part of an advanced decision.

Advanced statement

An advanced statement gives you the opportunity to put down in writing your more general lifestyle preferences, should you become unable to communicate these at a later date. It can cover day-to-day preferences such as what type of food and drink you like, clothes you like to wear, music, entertainment, bathing, who you would like to visit you, etc. It is a good place to write down any religious or spiritual beliefs you have and how you would like them to be honoured.

Although this is not legally binding, it does give your family and carers useful information about how you would like to live and be treated. It is also helpful to let your attorneys have this information if you have set up an LPA for health and care decisions as it allows them to make decisions for you that are consistent with your previous wishes.

Making a will

It is estimated that about a half of adults in the UK do not have a will – or do have one that is no longer valid. That means that they have no say over what happens to their estate if they die, and it would therefore be allocated or divided up according to strict intestacy rules.

This could present significant issues for people who are left behind, especially if they are not recognised in the intestacy rules, for example, a partner you live with or common law spouse, when you are neither married nor in a civil partnership, even if you have children together.

The process of making of a will is surprisingly easy and not too expensive. It can be done by a lawyer who can explain the technicalities and do the proper wording of the will and ensure that it is signed and witnessed in the correct way. It is easy to find local law firms that specialise in wills and probate and book an appointment.

There are other ways to do it not involving a lawyer. There are professional will writers (who would need to be a member of the Institute of Professional Will Writers), or there are some charities which will draft wills for free. Some banks will help you write a will, but you would need to check how much they charge for this service. It is also possible to write your own will, but it is important that it is done in the correct way with the required signatures, otherwise it may not be valid – so simply writing a list of your wishes on a piece of paper and signing it will not suffice.

It may not be the process that is getting in the way of people making a will, but uncertainty about the contents. Who do you leave it to? This can be a minefield for some people as their head may be saying one thing and their heart another. There may be fears of upsetting or offending people, and there may be a list of 'shoulds' and 'oughts' that you are grappling with. However, it is your life and your estate and you can do what you like with it. No one is obligated to leave it to their closest family, for example – it could be left to a whole mix of different people or charities of your choice. Making these difficult decisions is sadly part of adult life, and it is best thought through calmly and with enough time to consider it well.

Another part of the process is to decide who you would like to be your executor(s). These are people who are responsible for ensuring that your wishes in your will are carried out properly. This involves their time and effort, so it is best to seek their agreement first. Another aspect of this is to think about how old they are in relation to you, as you would need to work out the likelihood of you dying before they do.

There is a list of criteria that need to be met to ensure a will is valid. It is worth being aware of these, especially if you are doing a DIY will. People have to have mental capacity to sign their will, so it is too late to make a will after the loss of mental capacity, such as that caused by dementia. Another way to invalidate a previous will is by getting married or entering a civil partnership – in this case you would need to write another one. It is as well to do the same if you divorce or separate.

Planning a funeral

Perhaps the legacy of black and sombre Victorian funerals is stuck in the minds of many people and makes them a topic to avoid thinking about. However, there's a rather heartening sign in a local funeral director's window – 'Funerals, like birds, are all different and can be full of colour and song'.

What happens after you die is something that is worth thinking about in advance. One might debate who funerals are actually for – the deceased person or their families and friends left behind? Whichever way one looks at it, it is most likely that the remaining family and friends and other mourners would like to know that you had preferences about how your passing might be marked. Assuming you have left some money, then it is usually your estate that will pay for the funeral and any related gathering, so it reasonable to make some preferences about it known in advance and even have it planned.

If you decide on a funeral, you can plan it in great detail, e.g. to create a mood which is more celebratory than sombre or vice versa. Or you can leave that decision completely to others. Funeral companies are much more flexible than they used to be. Consider for example the options of burial, cremation, direct cremation and promession, or burial in a biodegradable box in a wood coffin versus a top-of-the-range solid oak coffin in a crypt. Promession uses liquid nitrogen to freeze-dry a dead body and then vibrates it so hard that it explodes into particles. The particles are then dried and mixed with soil.

Contrary to what a lot of people believe, one doesn't have to have a funeral at all. There is no legal requirement to do so. Some people dislike funerals so much that they request that one doesn't take place when they die. Some relatives feel the same and may make that decision themselves when their family member dies. Direct cremations are becoming increasingly popular – they are a lot cheaper to arrange and involve the funeral directors taking the coffin themselves to a crematorium for cremation. There is no service, and no one else attends. The ashes can be dealt with according to the family's wishes, including being collected by the family later so that they can have their own ashes ceremony at an appropriate place of their choosing.

It is also possible to arrange a DIY funeral without a funeral director, but there will still be fees for burial or cremation – more information on this is available via your local Council. It would require a lot of planning if you are not using any of the services of a funeral director. The official death registration processes would still have to be done, including the fees for this.

Regarding costs, many people are aware of how expensive even a fairly modest funeral is – often several thousand pounds. Some people plan for this by setting up a funeral payment plan in advance. One can compare prices of different funeral directors, and elements of the funeral can be made cheaper or more expensive depending on your choices for type of coffin, flowers, ceremonies, etc. Burials are generally more expensive than cremations. Instead of a religious ceremony, it can be led by friends and relatives themselves or by employing a non-denominational celebrant who will lead the ceremony according to your choices.

Loss and grieving

Types of loss

As we age, the chances of experiencing loss increase. Although we might automatically think this about losing a loved one, possibly a partner, family member or friend, there are other types of loss that surface with age. Not all are about significant people dying; some are situational (like loss of work, health, status, familiar environment), and some are more abstract, such as loss of choice, or loss of opportunity. Just because it is a less obvious loss doesn't mean it is not significant. There is no official list of 'valid losses' in life – everyone is different and sometimes a major loss for one person would be less significant for another. For example, some people are bemused by the depth of grief that a friend is experiencing after their beloved companion dog has died.

How we respond to loss

Our response to significant loss is grief. It is well known that many western cultures are uncomfortable about dealing with loss and grief. This can make the whole process that much more difficult for individuals who are grieving.

Elizabeth Kubler-Ross is a well-known author on this subject. She initially wrote about the five stages of death and dying, and many people are familiar with these: denial, anger, bargaining, depression and acceptance. She subsequently applied the same stages to loss and grief. She was dedicated to helping people understand what is happening to them at such a vulnerable time and to help others to support them as best they can. Her model is helpful, and it makes a lot of sense. For those of us who have been through a significant loss, we can look back and see variations on the themes of these five stages that happened to us. We can even more easily see it happening to others going through grief.

Kubler-Ross was keen to remove the misunderstandings about her 'stages' – and emphasised that there are many subtle ways in which any of the five stages can manifest for an individual. Also, they were not fixed milestones of a process of grieving that people predictably and neatly went through – they could occur in different orders, and some people rotate back and forth through different stages of grief in shorter or longer timescales. She wanted to point out human individuality, and not everyone adheres to strict models. We can't monitor someone's progress through sequential stages to see if they are doing it 'right' or 'on time'.

It is understandable, in our culture, that people who feel uncomfortable around loss and grief might want to compartmentalise grief into a neat package of controllable stages. It is an attempt to intellectualise and operationalise a potentially bewildering and devastating human experience. In a way, it is a cultural rendition of denial. This was not how Kubler-Ross intended her work to be understood. She wanted the culture to become more aware of the needs of the dying and the needs of the grieving.

So for us as individuals, what is useful is to appreciate the many varied responses to loss and to be understanding and accepting of them. It is worth becoming more aware of what might happen to us in grief, not just to have some self-compassion but also compassion for others.

Death and dying, grief and grieving are often hidden away behind closed curtains and doors, and behind cheerful, brave faces. We need to be more open-minded and open-hearted about it, however uncomfortable that feels. What a gift it is to be with someone whose world just fell through the floor, and hold a supportive space with them without the usual placating epithets ('you must be strong'; 'you're so brave'; 'X or Y wouldn't want to see you so upset', etc.).

Dealing with loss and grief

There are many helpful books and articles relating personal stories of how people have dealt with the most egregious of personal losses. Although reading about other people's grief at a time when you are going through your own may seem like the last thing you might want to consider, sometimes it is comforting to know that you are not alone in this. Each person gets through it in their own way, in their own time, and there is no 'how-to' guide that works for all. However, the following general points may be helpful.

Getting appropriate support

For overt losses, like the death of a loved one, there be a flurry of offers of help and support straight away, but these may dwindle over time. People usually want to be helpful, but getting the balance right is difficult to gauge. It is fine to ask for more or specific help from friends and family – or to ask them (kindly) to back off a bit and give you some space, if you need that. Don't underestimate the usefulness of professional support if that feels appropriate, as there are many therapists and counsellors who specialise in loss and bereavement.

For non-overt and potential losses, like anticipatory grief or more abstract losses, then it can be more difficult for other people to really understand what's going on for you. It is difficult enough for *you* to know what is happening – so getting professional help may be particularly helpful so you can feel supported and understood.

Self-compassion

There has been a lot of thinking about the concept of self-compassion in the last 15 years or so. Kristen Neff's book, 'Self Compassion' has a helpful approach to it and sees it as a mix of three strands:

- Self-kindness. It helps to fully appreciate how very tough this situation is and cut yourself a lot of slack. Purposely focus on what acts of self-kindness you can do for yourself – little things as well as the more substantial.
- Mindfulness. This is about acceptance and awareness of what is happening to you in each moment rather than over-identifying with it, denying it or running from it. Feelings come and they pass through, if you don't block them or grab onto them too much. There are many useful guides to mindfulness available these days, despite the concept not being at all new. Take from them what you find helpful.
- Common humanity. It changes our focus when we realise loss and grief are a common human experience – we are all vulnerable creatures on this planet, and awful things can happen to any one of us. No one is immune. We don't feel so separate or singled out when we realise we are all in this together and most of the difference is generally just timing and luck.

Anticipatory grief

Anticipatory grief is particularly difficult as the loss hasn't happened yet but feels like it is hovering around the next corner. When you (or a loved one) are given a serious diagnosis with a poor prognosis or great uncertainty, then it is understandable that you will conjure up various awful potential outcomes. This imagined horrendous future can completely take over your life. It is important to keep things more balanced and purposely train yourself to also focus on the here and now – what *is* okay now, what *is* working, what we *do have* in the present moment. It is easier said than done, but as Michel de Montaigne, the French Renaissance philosopher, once said, 'My life has been full of terrible misfortunes, most of which never happened'.

For anticipatory grief as well as situational and abstract losses, it can help to remember the three concentric circles about focus of control. In the outer circle, there are all the things we are concerned about; the middle circle contains that part that we have some influence over; and the inner circle contains the smaller portion that we also have control over. When we shift our focus to our circle of control and circle of influence, we feel we have more agency and feel less like a victim.

It takes time

We all know that time is a great healer, but having the patience and fortitude to stick it out is so hard. However, eventually things do get a little easier, no matter how unlikely that feels when we are in the thick of it. Over the course of time, some sort of acceptance will happen, even though we may be very changed by the experience of loss. For many people, it can also bring a new sense of meaning to our lives and our own sense of humanity.

Chapter 11

Additional resources

In this chapter, we first return to the personality theory referred to in earlier chapters and in particular its application to improving communication and decision making. Then we outline several more techniques and skills for managing some of the changes and problems associated with getting old: assertiveness, managing stress, writing life stories and expressive writing.

Preference theory and improving communication

One particularly useful application of preference theory is to understand and improve how we communicate with each other. People with different personality preferences tend to communicate in a way consistent with their preferences. It is not just the focus of the content of what we say; it is also the style in which we say it. This means that the more similar we are in terms of preferences, the easier it tends to be to for each person to be heard and understood. The reverse is also true – the more different we are, the more there are likely to be very different styles of communication which can result in misunderstandings and frustrations, especially if we are not aware of what is going on. There is no right or wrong in terms of communication – we just need to be more open to accepting the diversity of styles and become more flexible in our approach with people who are very different from us.

People with each pair of preferences tend to find the following differences a problem:

- between people who prefer Extraversion and those who prefer Introversion: need to talk versus need to be alone

- between people who prefer Sensing and those who prefer Intuition: focus on details and realism versus focus on general picture, links and speculation
- between people who prefer Thinking and those who prefer Feeling: being seen as unsympathetic and critical versus being seen as illogical and too agreeable
- between people who prefer Judging and those who prefer Perceiving: controlling and planning versus flexible and very open to change

Some strategies for managing (and preventing) communication problems between people with opposite preferences follow directly from the likely difficulties:

- people who prefer Extraversion with those who prefer Introversion: allow time for privacy and to reflect
- people who prefer Introversion with those who prefer Extraversion: explain need for time alone, allow for the other person's need to talk in order to clarify
- people who prefer Sensing with those who prefer Intuition: give the overall picture or purpose first, with relevant details later
- people who prefer Intuition with those who prefer Sensing: say a particular idea is speculative before saying what it is; include some detail
- people who prefer Thinking with those who prefer Feeling: include effects on people; begin with points of agreement
- people who prefer Feeling with those who prefer Thinking: include reasons and consequences; be concise
- people who prefer Judging with those who prefer Perceiving: allow for lots of flexibility in plans, style of working, etc. and for the other person's need not to be or feel controlled
- people who prefer Perceiving with those who prefer Judging: allow for some planning and structure and for the other person's need to control and decide

A closely related approach to communication is the four temperaments model, which we introduced in Chapter 7. Some implications of the four temperaments model for improving communication are:

- SPs (people who prefer both Sensing and Perceiving) need action, so if they see a practical problem that they want to do something about, stand aside! They also hate feeling trapped, so offer options and avoid pressurising.

- SJs (both Sensing and Judging) need tradition and structure, so are decisive and orderly, specific and detailed. They tend to focus on a task until it's finished and to dislike distractions. Otto Kroeger advised 'hit and run' when you want to suggest a change of plan to someone who prefers Sensing and Judging: speak concisely and leave quickly.
- NTs (both Intuition and Thinking) criticise to improve something or someone, and to analyse them, so they like debating, solving problems impersonally and using complicated theories. Therefore, offer (well-reasoned) criticism, be prepared to have your competence tested, and try not to take criticism personally. Indeed, it may well be a compliment: your idea or behaviour is worth bothering with.
- NFs (both Intuition and Feeling) need to develop themselves as people and to help others to do the same. They provide and thrive on encouragement, warmth and approval, and they tend to take criticism personally. Their approach is naturally collaborative.

Preference theory and making decisions

Preference theory assumes that we make our best decisions using both Thinking and Feeling, but giving the most weight to the one we prefer. Thus people who prefer Feeling can use their non-preference for Thinking to list points for and against, then their preference for Feeling to say which of the points matter most, then Feeling again to make the decision. Conversely, people who prefer Thinking are likely to find the analytic listing of points and arguments most natural, but can also include their emotional reactions to each point, then come back to their Thinking again to make the decision.

Another framework for making decisions based on the theory is to use four preferences:

Sensing: what are the relevant facts and details?

Intuition: what are the possible ways, however speculative and unlikely, of interpreting these facts? And are any models or theories relevant?

Thinking: what are the consequences of each choice, short- and long-term? What are the arguments? What's logical?

Feeling: what are the probable effects on each person involved? What are the priorities here? Which do I like most?

The theory implies putting the most effort into the stages associated with our non-preferences (because they are likely to be less developed) and applying our preferences last (because they are likely to be more trustworthy).

Assertiveness skills

Assertiveness can be defined as respecting your own rights and the rights of other people. It can be defined in terms of those rights (e.g. those listed in the next section) and as skills, e.g. saying no, making requests, giving and receiving compliments and giving and receiving criticism.

If you want to try being more assertive, we suggest looking out first for times when you are not assertive and regret it. For example, you might observe one or more of the following:

- you said yes or behaved in a way that 'said' yes when you'd rather have said no
- you didn't ask someone for something when you'd rather you had asked
- you rejected a compliment when you actually liked it and believed it was genuine
- you didn't give someone a genuine compliment when you wanted to

Take one of these exchanges, for example the time you'd rather have said no, and analyse it:

1 Write down what you'd rather have said, ideally finding a key phrase. (You may wish to change this key phrase later as a result of the other steps.)
2 Consider the possible costs of saying no.
3 Consider the possible benefits of saying no.
4 With this person in that situation, which are more important to you: the benefits or the costs?

It can be very clarifying to rehearse the likely interaction with a mirror, recording device, friend or group (carefully chosen!) for practising the assertive skills of everyone in it.

Next, if your ideas about the likely benefits exceed the costs, consider actually saying no to that person the next time the opportunity arises, using your key phrase. The word 'no' itself can be particularly powerful too. Another option is to create the opportunity to be assertive: 'You asked me yesterday to help you with X and I've thought hard . . .' or 'Earlier you asked me to do X for you and I said I would. I've thought about it and changed my mind'. There are many other variations, which will depend on the particular situation where you want to say no and also on the relationship with the person you are saying no to. Anne Dickson's book *A Woman in Your Own Right* (which applies just as well to men) includes many excellent examples of the skills in action.

Another way that assertiveness can be used is to analyse a problem from the perspective of a list of assertive rights such as the one given later. The usual way assertive rights are described is for oneself only, but the format here, devised by Meg Bond in her book *Stress and Self-awareness. A guide for nurses*, conveys in a very clear way that assertiveness is about respect for the same rights in other people too.

Deciding whether you agree or not with each assertive right may also clarify your values. An exercise you may wish to try is to consider each pair of rights in turn. How easy or difficult do you find it to accept this right as generally true for first other people and then yourself? The rights can be particularly helpful when you are upset or angry to realise that your reaction is or may be out of proportion to the event apparently causing it.

Assertive rights for oneself and others

1 I have the right to be treated with respect, **and** others have the right to be treated with respect.
2 I have the right to express my thoughts, opinions and values, **and** others have the right to express their thoughts, opinions and values.
3 I have the right to express my feelings, **and** others have the right to express their feelings.
4 I have the right to say 'no' without feeling guilty, **and** others have the right to say 'no' without feeling guilty.
5 I have the right to be successful, **and** others have the right to be successful.
6 I have the right to make mistakes, **and** others have the right to make mistakes.
7 I have the right to change my mind, **and** others have the right to change their minds.

8 I have the right to say that I don't understand, **and** others have the right to say they don't understand.
9 I have the right to ask for what I want, **and** others have the right to ask for what they want.
10 I have the right to decide for myself whether or not I am responsible for another person's problems, **and** others have the right to decide for themselves whether or not they are responsible for another person's problems.
11 I have the right to choose not to assert myself, **and** others have the right to choose not to assert themselves.

Managing stress

Some signs of too much stress are:

* *on thoughts and emotions*: difficulty concentrating, being anxious, irritable or bored, low mood
* *on the body*: tight throat, aches, dry mouth, tics, frequent urination
* *on behaviour*: accidents, drug misuse, criticising, sleep difficulties

It's important to note that some of these signs of stress may be caused by *illness* and may therefore need medical attention. Moreover, another sign, unfortunately, is ignoring such signs. Ideally, we would notice them early and take action to reduce or remove them, but being stressed is itself distracting. The advantages of early action are obvious: less energy wasted and less damage done. Working out the source(s) of stress, internal and external, may also be more feasible.

Preference theory and stress

The theory of personality preferences introduced in Chapter 7 states that the activities and circumstances which are enjoyable for people with some preferences are stressful for those with the opposite preferences.

Extraversion – not much happening; not enough contact with people (even though most do need some time on their own)
Introversion – not enough time for reflection or for oneself
Sensing – vagueness and abstract theory

> Intuition – routine, repetitive and detailed activities
> Thinking – lack of logic, intense emotions
> Feeling – conflict and criticism, discourtesy
> Judging – lack of plans, and changes of plan
> Perceiving – restrictions on autonomy, few or no options

Coping with stress

A three-stage model of coping with stress is:

> Stage 1: Monitor your signs of too much or too little stimulation, especially *early* warnings
> Stage 2: Choose one or more coping strategies
> Stage 3: Try them out, monitoring the effects

Choosing one or more coping strategies is currently a matter of personal experiment, although some strategies work well for most people and are therefore more likely to be worth trying. They include exercise (Chapter 1), sleep (Chapter 3), expressive writing (this chapter) and relaxation.

Physical relaxation

Physical relaxation is a direct way of coping with stress, both immediately and preventively, and instructions/guidelines are widely available. Two 10-minute sessions of progressive relaxation a day seem to have a beneficial and cumulative effect. However, sometimes attempting to relax is itself stressful. Several factors can make a difference: e.g. some people prefer a well-lit room, others a dark one; some respond best to several two- or three-minute sessions, and so on. Moreover, someone can try too hard to relax or may be afraid of losing control of certain images or emotions. Relaxation can also be boring and therefore stressful.

A simple relaxation technique from yoga is to:

1   Make yourself comfortable. Take two or three deep breaths through your nose. Then place one of your index fingers on the point between your eyebrows, with the thumb on one nostril, middle finger on the other.
2   Closing your left nostril, breathe in slowly and deeply through the right.

3   Closing your right nostril, breathe out slowly through the left.
4   Keeping the right nostril closed, breathe in through the left.
5   Closing the left nostril, breathe out through the right.

You can breathe in to (say) a count of three, hold for two, out to six – but ideally, find your own rhythm. A further refinement of the instructions is that when you've breathed out, pause and wait until you want to breathe in – until it 'feels right'.

Writing life stories

Many people find it helpful to explore their life stories. They discover something surprising and useful and make more sense of their life and of themselves. Others have no interest, sometimes because their lives feel too traumatic and are best left alone.

The process of exploring and analysing life stories can be emotional. If you become 'caught up' or stuck in an emotion, distraction techniques like counting backwards in sevens from (say) 300, or breathing slowly and deeply, can be effective for regaining enough composure to continue reflecting and analysing, or to stop.

A simple approach to writing a life story is to just write, say, three pages. You might also try writing in the third person, from the perspective of someone who knows you well. Another option is to use a structure, e.g. chronological, places you've lived, life events you see as pivotal or close relationships.

The life story interview

Dan McAdams developed a more elaborate system: the life story interview, in which the interviewee (who can be the same person as the interviewer) is asked first to think about their life as if it were a book with chapters, and then to identify each chapter and outline its contents, like a plot summary. Next, she or he is asked to describe eight key scenes from their story, each depicting one of the following events: a high point, a low point, a turning point, earliest memory, important childhood episode, important adolescent episode, important adult episode and one other important episode.

There are five further stages in the full life story interview. Briefly, they are describing the biggest challenge faced by the interviewee and how they met it; the character with the most positive effect on their life and the one with the most negative effect; an account of where the story is going, for example main goals, dreams and fears; questions on values and religious and political beliefs; and, finally, identifying a single integrative theme.

At each stage, the interviewer can vary in how probing they are and in their use of theory to guide their questions. In analysing your answers, the key question is 'what does this aspect say about who I am and who I might be?' For example, a theme might be that you have been faced with many obstacles but have resiliently overcome them, and you might choose to continue in your life with this theme, or refine it, add to it or reject it.

Exploring life stories can stimulate feelings of nostalgia which can be seen as pointless or detrimental. However, nostalgia can have positive effects such as strengthening our sense of identity and reminding us of how we have coped with a problem before. Curiously, such effects quite often occur a few days after reminiscing rather than immediately.

Reflecting in a nostalgic way may lead to you feeling guilty about things you did (or failed to do) many years before. In turn, you may feel you should atone in some way. Before you act, please consider the idea that your good actions may outweigh those you feel guilty about and thus make the case for action less compelling.

In addition, please also consider who the action is for. A way of doing this is to apply assertive rights (see earlier in this chapter) to both yourself and anyone else you are inclined to involve. For example, 'I have the right to make mistakes' **and** 'Others have the right to make mistakes' or 'I have the right to be treated with respect' **and** 'Others have the right to be treated with respect'. Does your possible action treat the other(s) with respect? Might they have forgotten about what you did or didn't do or not want to be reminded?

Expressive writing

Expressive writing is an effective way of managing stress and improving health for many people. Generally, it has beneficial effects through increasing a sense of perspective, calmness and control, and clarifying emotions, thoughts, wishes and values, which in turn tend to lead to better decisions and actions. Moreover, it is inexpensive, portable and private and has a low risk of negative effects.

The following method is based on the extensive research on expressive writing. There are four steps:

Step one is to write freely about a preoccupation, problem, question or event. The research on the effects of doing this has been on a wide range of topics from traumatic events like being in an earthquake to positive ones like new and good things in your life. Decisions, reactions to a news item or a memory are other possibilities – anything that you find puzzling, troubling or interesting.

Write for yourself alone, and aim to write for at least 15 minutes.

A variation for step one is 'freewriting'. This is writing without stopping, censoring or editing (you can shred it later) about whatever comes to mind, either generally or about a particular topic. Put grammar, spelling and punctuation aside. Write anything, but keep writing. Write for at least 15 minutes, including things like 'I'm stuck' or 'this is silly'.

Freewriting comes easily to some people and for others develops with practice or doesn't suit them. If you're writing using a computer, you may feel freer not looking at the screen.

Step two is to analyse what you've written. In freewriting particularly, you'll probably find some repetition and lots of uninteresting stuff but also some useful and sometimes surprising bits. Underline those. You're writing and analysing to clarify and discover what you mean, feel, value, think and want. The following questions can be useful as prompts:

1   What emotions/feelings/thoughts that may be useful have you written down? Are you reminded of others?
2   What actually happened (specifically)?
3   How might other people have reacted in your position?
4   How would you like to have reacted?

Step two is meant to be very different in 'feel' from step one: thoughtful, considered and detached rather than spontaneous and free. Being kind to yourself about what you've written is a helpful idea for some people.

Step three is to write a list of possible actions to take about the problem or issue you've written about. These can range from the practical and easily achievable to the fanciful and wildly unlikely to happen. They can include a change of attitude on your part as well as things you might say or do.

Step four is to consider the arguments for and against each possible action. For example, is it legal? What are the likely effects on others and on you, short-term and long-term?

Or you could apply the steps of writing freely and analysing to the actions or discuss them with someone you trust. It can be particularly useful if this person is significantly different in personality from you, e.g. someone more logical, if you tend to focus more on how you and others feel or vice versa.

Risks of expressive writing

A risk of expressive writing in some people's view is that it is self-indulgent and can lead to 'wallowing in misery' and your mood spiralling down. The four steps are designed to counter this: being stuck and the opposite risk of premature action are both countered.

Further, someone else may read what you've written and react badly. Solutions include writing PRIVATE at the top, putting it in a locked drawer or shredding it.

You may feel worse after expressive writing. There is something about putting things into words, spoken or written, which can have this effect, especially short-term. However, the positive and longer-term effects of writing in this way are significant: for example, greater clarity and better health, as shown by fewer visits to a health centre in the six months after doing it, and lower levels of stress hormones. Thus it is a matter of balancing risks against benefits.

An example of freewriting with commentary

Step one (abbreviated): write freely

My hamstring hurts again. That's 3 ½ months of several times of apparent recovery and then not right again. This happens every few days. Feel despairing, very fed up and old. I've been disciplined and patient (for me) and it seemed fine. Will it ever be right again? Have I damaged it so that keeping fit, well what counts as fit at my age, is impossible?

Step two: analysis

Note: If you used the technique of freewriting in step one, it's probably best to underline the potentially useful bits before doing step two.

I do feel despairing at times but even if it's a serious injury people recover from much worse and I know that, just forget it sometimes.

So I'm being overdramatic and catastrophizing and this is very familiar where injuries are concerned.

This injury is uncomfortable rather than painful. On the other hand the repetitive slight injuries may be cumulatively damaging.

Also, I'm very lucky to have played football for nearly all my life with only occasional minor injuries so even if this is the end of my football it's been good.

Step three: possible actions

1 Try a different physio? Ideally I'd go to see Paul.
2 Let go of playing football.
3 Ask my GP (a rugby player) to recommend a physio.
4 Be even more gradual in how I build up to full recovery.
5 Buy an exercise ball to sit on.
6 Look up lower back injuries and treatments because I'd forgotten that they can lead to discomfort away from the back.
7 I do slouch and sprawl a lot (what are sofas for?) so posture and back stretcher.
8 It may be significant that while I can do lots of press-ups I'm weak at lunges. Core muscles?
9 Similarly, it may be as simple as that I've been doing too many lunges and squats; I do tend (to put it kindly) to do appealing new things too enthusiastically.
10 Operation?

Step four (abbreviated): decide which actions to do and how and when

Action 2 is still too soon and premature to explore it, and 1 and 3 are for if the others don't work. Actions 4 and 8 need patience so are difficult, but vital, I suspect, and 10 is silly and impatient. The rest I'll do, gently, starting today. Discipline! But do them with TV or music.

Suggestions for further reading

Rowan Bayne (2013) *The Counsellor's Guide to Personality: Understanding Preferences, Motives and Life Stories*. Palgrave Macmillan.

Linda Berens (2000) *Understanding Yourself and Others: An Introduction to Temperament*.: Telos Publications.

Patrizia Collard (2014) *The Little Book of Mindfulness, 10 minutes a day to less stress, more peace*. Gaia Books.

Rangan Chatterjee (2018) *The Four Pillar Plan: How to Relax, Eat, Move and Sleep Your Way to a Longer, Healthier Life*. Penguin.

Anne Dickson (2012) *A Woman in Your Own Right: Assertiveness and You*. Quartet.

Alex Linley (2008) *Average to A+. Realising Strengths in Yourself and Others*.: CAPP Press.

Muir Gray (2015) *Sod 70! The Guide to Living Well*. Bloomsbury.

Phil Hammond (2015) *Staying Alive: How to Get the Best from the NHS*. Quercus.

Otto Kroeger & Janet M. Thuesen (1988) *Type Talk*. Delacorte Press.

Elisabeth Kubler-Ross & David Kessler (2014) *On Grief and Grieving*. Simon & Schuster.

Kathryn Mannix (2017) *With the End in Mind: How to Live and Die Well*. William Collins.

Michael Mosley (2018) *The Fast 800: How to Combine Rapid Weight Loss and Intermittent Fasting for Long Term Health*. Short Books.

Marion Shoard (2017) *How to Handle Later Life*. Amaranth Books Ltd., 2nd ed.

Tim Spector (2015) *The Diet Myth*. Weidenfeld & Nicolson.

Index